Honest Doubt – Real Faith

Also by Justyn Rees

Love Your Neighbour – For God's Sake

Honest Doubt – Real Faith

A true story of lost faith recovered

Justyn Rees

Hodder & Stoughton
LONDON SYDNEY AUCKLAND

First published in Great Britain in 1999

10 9 8 7 6 5 4 3 2 1

British Library Cataloguing in Publication Data
A record for this book is available from the British Library

ISBN 0 340 74576 2

Typeset by Avon Dataset Ltd, Bidford-on-Avon, Warks

Printed and bound in Great Britain by
Clays Ltd, St Ives plc

Hodder and Stoughton Ltd
A Division of Hodder Headline PLC
338 Euston Road
London NW1 3BH

Justyn Rees and his wife Joy live in British Columbia in western Canada where they direct Upstream Christian Initiatives. Their work is to find practical and creative ways to help others enter into a loving relationship with God, and so with their neighbours. Justyn was formerly Director of the Hildenborough Evangelistic Trust Ltd, in south-east England.

The identities of some people and certain circumstances have been disguised in order to protect their privacy.

Contents

1

Bottom of the Pit

There are few places on earth as gloomy as the west coast
of Scotland in the autumn.

From where I sat in my caravan I could see across the
white caps which filled the bay to the ruins of the Castle of
Doon, then beyond to the purple grey of the Cuillin Hills.
The rain assaulted my windows and the wind moaned and
snarled around, occasionally shaking my frail dwelling as a
terrier shakes a rabbit.

It was useless to attempt to keep the stove alight, for the
wind had the upper hand and I feared the possibility of
gassing myself. Death. I had never had cause to fear it
before.

An otter leaped through the waves not twenty feet from
where I sat. What right had he to enjoy the storm, rolling
and diving and somersaulting as though the whole force of
nature was kicking up its heels just for him? The fun had
gone out of life for me.

I was alone. No one inhabited that desolate stretch of
coast on the Isle of Skye. The only company I had were the
sheep, the gulls and the otter. There was no God to talk to,
so prayer offered no companionship.

A shiver shook me as I noticed that the light was fading.
Another night. If there were disembodied souls on the loose,

as many thereabouts believed there were, then this would be their chance to bid me join them.

But if there was no God, then perhaps some comfort was to be derived from the likelihood that there were no spirits either, disembodied or otherwise. Yet who could tell what there might be lurking out there in the darkness?

'Beware of the equinoctial gales,' the old lady at the post office had warned me, with a wild Highland look in her eyes. We had reached the equinox all right, and now the night was overreaching the day. The Indian summer which had enticed me so far north looked like turning to a Scottish winter overnight.

Six months had now elapsed since I had come to the unwilling realisation that I no longer believed in God. Like a sick animal I had longed to crawl into a hole to hide my demise from the inquisitive stares of the world. At last I was away in the deepest hole I knew. Six hundred miles from my home in south-east England; no telephone, no friends, no Christians, no responsibilities, no nothing.

Peace at last. But peace it was not, for the absence of distractions only emphasised the absence of reality, the one reality that had filled my life till then, God himself.

That night sleep blew away with the storm. Reading was difficult, for the lamp was struggling for survival. If you have ever spent a night trying to sleep in an express train which is attempting to make up lost time, then you may be able to sympathise. The van swayed and rattled, and derailment seemed inevitable. But for the precaution I had taken of attaching the hitch to the car and tying everything down to solid rock, I must surely have blown away.

Thoughts were all I had to pass the time and I was a prisoner, shut up with them till morning. So I had been wrong all those years. I had fooled others, as I myself had been deceived, into following a faith which was no more than wishful thinking. My parents were wrong. My father was dead, having wasted his life on falsehood. At least with no afterlife he would never have had to face up to his mistake.

How was I to raise my children? Could I admit to them that I had been wrong to teach them to pray? Perhaps I could quietly let them come to their own conclusions as they were rapidly doing over Santa Claus. But what was I to teach them instead? What would be my new basis for teaching them right and wrong? What hope could I offer them for survival in a world with no one in control? Perhaps it would have been better if I had never had children at all.

How was I to earn a living? For the past seven years I had managed a Christian retreat centre and had travelled the land as an itinerant preacher. But how could I go on preaching a gospel I no longer believed? How could I run a faith enterprise trusting a God who was no longer there?

How could I face my friends again? 'A traitor to the cause' they would justifiably call me. I'd be an embarrassment to all who might ever hear about the preacher who gave up his faith. And what if there really were a God after all (and how I wished there were)? Then I would be living my life as a constant insult to his very existence, and by my own existence I would be leading others astray also. Why couldn't I have been a private, everyday Christian instead of being the one at the front? I could sympathise with Peter, who stepped out of his boat in a storm to walk by faith to Jesus. Poor fellow! He too had had an audience of all his friends to witness his humiliation as he sank beneath the waves.

The equinoctial gale vented its spite on my intrusion. 'Lord save me!' I cried. The lamp gave up the struggle and went out, and I saw to my relief the first grey of an unwilling dawn. I sank beneath the waves of exhaustion to blessed oblivion.

2

A Clear Blue Sky

Hildenborough Hall stood like a medieval castle crowning a shoulder of the North Downs in the heart of the Kentish countryside, the garden of England.

Though the place had been built as recently as 1929, the architect had spared no expense to give the impression of grandeur normally associated with the numerous 'ancient piles' that litter the British landscape. White marble hallways led from a studded oak front door through a labyrinth of reception rooms. A drawing room overlooked the croquet lawn and rose gardens. The oak-panelled library, with its heavy stone fireplace, housed shelves of leather-backed books. Press the right button and a wall of books swung outwards, revealing a secret room. A complete barn of Tudor origin had been transported to the site, where in its reconstructed form it made an impressive dining hall. There, around the massive-beamed fireplace, silver-service meals were served by black-tied waiters. A spacious conference room looked out over the kidney-shaped swimming pool, past the ramparts of the terrace to the distant landscape beyond.

Situated as it was in over fifty acres of land, it was hard to realise that London was just over the hill; ten million people within an hour's drive.

Suddenly and unexpectedly I became 'Lord of the Manor'. One day we were in British Columbia trying to find employment, and a week later we were five thousand miles away with a multi-million-dollar slice of real estate to administer, thirty staff members to organise and twenty-five years of goodwill on which to capitalise.

The sudden change had been occasioned by the death of my father, Tom Rees, a giant of a preacher, described by some as Britain's Billy Graham. He had founded Hildenborough Hall the same year as he founded me, soon after the Second World War. Using the conference centre as his base of operations, he initiated evangelistic crusades throughout the UK and across Canada and the US. He left big footprints to fill. The day after his funeral, the Hildenborough Board of Trustees met and invited me to take over the direction of the work. I would have been foolish to have declined, yet I was too young and inexperienced to know that I was too young and inexperienced.

For the first couple of years we kept the established programme ticking over just as it always had. Then one day, as we walked up and down the half-mile driveway, Joy and I discussed change.

'What we should do, Joy, is to run it as a kind of Christian country club, but gear it for young people.'

Joy's eyes lit up in enthusiasm.

'We could make it feel a bit like a home, albeit a big one. I'll run the kitchen and housekeeping side of the operation and you can be the front man.'

Joy, in addition to qualifying as a registered nurse, was a domestic scientist. Because of her exceptional talents in the kitchen, the bathroom scales have long been my worst enemy.

'We must offer a consistent programme, so we'll open every weekend throughout the year.'

'But that would mean discontinuing all the revenue-earning private conference bookings. How many visitors do you think we'd have on an average weekend?'

'Maybe twenty-five? What do you think?'

'I have no idea. So we'll have to be flexible in the way we cater.'

'Young people are too informal in their lifestyles to book up in advance, so let's advertise that all they have to do is to arrive and we will find them a place to sleep.'

'But how will they afford the fees?' Joy is ever the practical one in our marriage.

'Some have lots of money and some have none. They can come on a donation basis.'

'Who are you kidding? You'll never make ends meet that way.'

That autumn we started the Hildenborough Open House programme. I was wrong to anticipate twenty-five guests. A hundred and ten showed up the first weekend, and we never dropped below seventy-five.

On Saturday evenings we laid on a programme for non-residents. Several hundred would cram themselves into the conference lounge for a concert, a 'cinema seminar', as we termed a discussion on a current movie, or a celebrity evening with some well-known personality.

Joy was run off her feet keeping things going behind the scenes, and I felt like a juggler with too many balls in the air as I sought to give leadership to the whole operation.

'We need help!'

* * *

Max Sinclair, my cousin, was tall, lean and athletic, with a magnificent ginger beard. His wife, Sue, would accord with much the same description, but for the beard. As Joy and I had been, they were out of the country when the call came to join the team at Hildenborough. Max, a chartered accountant, was working for a firm of accountants with a branch in Nairobi, Kenya. There they enjoyed the great outdoors, spending all the time they could away from the office exploring the game parks or climbing Mount Kenya.

I ruined their freedom.

Dear Max and Sue,
It's high time you came back to the UK. We're missing you.
Hildenborough is going well and there is no end to the scope for expansion. Please consider joining us as fellow evangelists. We need you.
Much love,
Justyn and Joy

Dear Justyn and Joy,
We like it in Kenya and have no intention of returning to the UK. Anyway, I am an accountant, not an evangelist.
Etc., etc.
Love,
Max and Sue

Dear Max and Sue,
We'll pray about it.
Etc., etc.
Love,
Justyn and Joy

Dear Justyn and Joy,

Our appointment in Nairobi has unexpectedly been terminated.

We'll be home next month and I'm bored with figures. Do you still need us?

Love,

Max and Sue

And so the Sinclairs came to Hildenborough.

Together, Max and I started an outreach programme into high schools.

We bought an old double-decker bus. The top deck we converted into a coffee lounge to which we could invite kids during the lunch hour. Downstairs served as a mobile movie theatre. 'Bertha' we called her on good days, and on bad days we called her every name in the book. One bright October morning stands out in my memory as one of the bad days.

We were headed for a large high school in Rickmansworth. It was Max's turn to drive, and as we trundled through the rush-hour traffic of north London we asked each other the same question we had asked a thousand times: 'Why do we do this sort of thing?' The school turned out to be huge and forbidding, closely resembling a prisoner of war camp. Though we had visited many schools, we never quite got over the cold terror which inevitably gripped us whenever we approached school gates.

On this occasion the terror was just as cold as ever. The gates, however, appeared to be narrower than usual. I suppose they must have been narrower; at least, they were before our visit. As we reached the point of no return between the gates, there was a terrible sound which only survivors of the *Titanic* could fully appreciate. We were stuck, wedged between two brick pillars. The exit and, more importantly at 8.30 in the morning, the entrance to the school was totally blocked.

The staff were in the school. The pupils were outside, and Max and I were wedged like a cork in a bottle in the middle. Cheers were coming from behind from a hundred scholars, delighted with the unexpected excuse to be late for class. Worry wrinkled the brow of the school principal who had been looking out for our arrival and now came running to see what had gone wrong. Max's brow was running with perspiration and my sides were aching with mirth.

There was nothing for it but to give Bertha the gas and see if she could break free by brute force. The gears ground and bit as the wheels clawed for traction. The brick pillars protested briefly, then gave up the struggle and collapsed in a cloud of dust and rubble. We were in and, judging from the tumult behind, we were heroes! Even Joshua didn't stage a more spectacular arrival in Jericho.

The principal's welcome was, shall we say, restrained. 'Mr Rees, Mr Sinclair, meet Mr Rodrick,' he introduced us to the religious education teacher. The principal's welcome had been cordial in comparison with the glassy stare with which this 'theologian' fixed us. He clearly did not approve of buses, evangelical Christians, and Max and me in particular.

Wishing the end of the world would intervene, we set up our amplifying equipment in preparation for the assembly. When all six hundred students had silently assembled on the far side of the closed stage curtains, we heard Mr Rodrick's guarded introduction.

'Some gentlemen have come to visit our school today and they are going to sing some songs about . . . ah . . . Jesus.'

The curtains drew aside and as the kids realised that the 'gentlemen' were none other than the demolishers of their school gates, cheers arose. We were in!

Fifteen minutes later we were guided down congested corridors to Mr Rodrick's sixth form (or grade 12) religious education class.

'I must warn you that you won't find them very sympathetic to your brand of religion,' he breathed as we entered the room.

The hubbub died away and all eyes were turned on the visitors.

'Good morning, 6A,' said our host.

'Good morning, sir,' droned back the opposition.

'Mr Rees and Mr Sinclair have come from Hildenborough Hall, a Christian conference centre, to speak to us about their views on Christianity. I have asked them to speak to you for the first fifteen minutes and then it will be over to you to ask them questions.'

Religious education, far from being banned in British schools as it is in Canada and the US, is a required part of the curriculum by the law of the land. But it has always been a source of amazement to me that agnostics and even atheists get appointed to teach the subject. Imagine a maths teacher who suggests that one plus one equals two or possibly three or maybe nothing at all!

Max was the first to bat. He told them how his faith in Jesus Christ had become real while at university in Durham. He spoke of his training as a chartered account-ant and his subsequent work in Nairobi. The students

11

seemed genuinely impressed that he would give up a promising career in favour of becoming an evangelist.

Then it was my turn.

I recounted how my faith had grown through a time of severe doubts while I was in the fifth form at school. I spoke frankly of the struggle I had experienced trying to reconcile the theory of evolution with Genesis chapter 1.

It was a scientist, I told them, who helped restore my faith while speaking of the remarkable similarities which exist between the Bible's account of the order of creation and the order which scientists now recognise.

Ths sixth form students regarded me quizzically. Rather than dwell too deeply on the peripheral issues, I homed in on the essential of the Christian faith, the resurrection of Jesus. 'Where did the body go?' I asked them. They made the usual suggestions.

'The disciples removed it.'

'But why?' I countered. 'And why did so many of them subsequently give their lives for something they knew deep down to be a hoax?'

'The Roman soldiers stole the coffin.'

'Again, why? When Christianity became an embarrassment to Rome, why didn't they publish abroad what they had done with the corpse?'

Finally, the cynical sixth offered the conclusion that it must have been the Jewish leaders themselves who removed Jesus' body. They had no motives to suggest, neither could they explain the Jews' oversight in failing to produce the body, thereby killing off Christianity in its infancy. 'How could they have overlooked so obvious a solution to their embarrassment when rumours of a resurrection started to circulate?'

My conclusion was that Jesus rose from the dead, and if he rose then his claims had to be taken seriously.

Then the questions started. They were the same questions which were served up in various guises in almost every discussion class we attended. They came at us six or eight times a day in class after class. 'Who made God?' 'Who was Cain's wife?' 'Hasn't science disproved religion?' 'Jesus was an astronaut from another planet.' 'How could a good God allow so much suffering in the world?' And so on. I knew all the standard answers and could win almost any argument. Having been through serious doubts myself when I was their age, I found no difficulty in sympathising with their difficulty in believing. The 'simply believe' merchants irritated me, too.

I was glad that my time of doubting God was behind me. My faith had graduated from a hand-me-down inheritance from my parents to a faith of my own. Doubting had been a necessary transition from one to the other. And now I was so well rehearsed in the facts of the faith that nothing could ever shake me again.

There was a sleepy-looking fellow sitting somewhere near the back of the class who thus far had contributed nothing to the debate. He raised an eyebrow, a hand and a vital question.

'All that you have been telling us is from the distant past or from the realms of religious theory. Why do you believe today and what is the relevance of this to us now?'

Max and I shared with him the reality of God's friendship in day-to-day affairs, of answered prayers, of the sense of peace which comes in difficult circumstances, knowing God is in control, of the purpose knowing God gives to life and the way he guides our decisions and circumstances.

'If God is watching over you so carefully, why did he let you demolish our gateposts this morning?'

The bell allowed us to escape from the laughter.

'He who puts ten men to work does more than he who tries to do the work of ten men.'

There was so much opportunity in schools that we resolved to multiply ourselves. We started a small school of evangelism offering a one-year on-the-job training. The idea was that we could both prepare people for the ministry of evangelism and provide a resource of talented young people to do the work.

'PACE – A Practical Adventure in Contemporary Evangelism' was the way we advertised the opportunity to prospective students. When we put them to work in the schools, we explained to the teachers that PACE stood for 'A Practical Approach to Christian Education'. The kids in school understood it to be a rock band called PACE who also doubled as a drama group, but had some strange religious ideas.

The first year was fraught with teething troubles. Eighteen young people enrolled. They saw themselves as students, and most acted accordingly. We had advertised it as a school of evangelism, and 'school' implied classes to learn to evangelise rather than responsibilities to do it. We became so absorbed in teaching how to evangelise that we had little time or energy left for actual evangelism.

So the next year we invited people to join us as members of an evangelistic team, and we promised to train them but made no mention of a school of evangelism. The result was a most interesting gathering of talented people. Bob Frasier came from Messiah College in Pennsylvania, bringing with him real musical expertise to lift a bunch of amateurs out of mediocrity.

Heidi Kaluzny came originally from California with a band called the Contemporaries. She was so struck by the needs of British young people that she jumped ship from the Contemporaries and joined PACE, contributing glamour and personality.

Dave Gladwin was from Reading in Berkshire, England. He brought destruction. Everything he touched broke. We visited a music store and a rack of guitars collapsed. He helped with the dishes at Hildenborough and a pile of best china plates disintegrated. On one occasion, while tuning up his guitar in preparation for a school assembly, Dave fell backwards through the curtains and off the front of the stage, landing in a sea of cross-legged students who were eagerly awaiting the start of the show. But everyone loved Dave.

Harold Heath was from Wigan in the north of England and brought stability and wit. Ellen, from Chino in California, was a story-teller and actress who could have the kids on the edge of their seats. Phil Taylor from Crowborough in Sussex brought nothing but a heart for evangelism, but soon found he had a natural sense of rhythm. He set to and mastered the primitive art of drumming.

Having an international team was not without its hazards. We had to interpret the language, for a start. 'Make yourself at home', in the context of an English home, does not mean help yourself to whatever is in the refrigerator and put your feet on the coffee table. Specific words also have different meanings on opposite sides of the Atlantic. Bob arrived at a school one morning, having downed his standard three cups of coffee, to find himself in urgent need of personal relief. He grabbed a passing student and, recognising that there was no time to lose, demanded, so he supposed, directions to the appropriate facility. 'Take me to the head.' The startled youngster led him up the hallway and pointed to a door marked in impressive lettering 'The Head'. Not pausing even to wonder if it was intended for boys or girls, he rushed through the door into the hallowed presence of the school principal, or 'Head Master'.

PACE soon developed amazing rapport with young people in the schools. After a week of visiting the religious education classes, leading the morning assemblies and laying on lunch-hour concerts, they were accepted. An invitation at the end of the week to 'Come on over to our place' was positively received, and dozens would come to Hildenborough Hall during the following weekends.

It quickly became obvious that we couldn't all do everything, so we adopted the principle of division of labour. Max gave leadership to PACE, brandishing a bass guitar and exuding goodwill and humour. That left me free to lead the residential work at the conference centre. I disliked the office work and general administration, so resorted to the art of delegation. I identified all the things I liked doing least and wrote them up in a job description with the grand title of 'Office Administrator' as a bait. I then set out to find someone gullible enough to take the job. Felicity Lane took the bait, swallowed the hook and felt called by the Lord to do so. To crown it all, I got the credit for sound management practice!

But there was still a missing dimension: maturity. We were all in our mid-twenties and as green as peppers.

Quintin Carr had worked for the Scripture Union for forty years. In recent years he had suffered a couple of heart attacks, so, as he always said, he lived with 'one foot in the grave and the other on a banana skin'. This disability shut him up to do the very thing he loved most. He could leave the paperwork to Felicity Lane and was free to spend his time with young people. We adopted him into the family and, as he was three times the average age of the rest of the team, we dubbed him 'Grandpa'.

Grandpa made it his business to get to know the name of every guest – no small feat when you consider his age and the eighty new names and faces to be memorised every week. His ability probably stemmed from a life-long habit of learning a verse from the Bible every day. He treated his daily verse as a 'Password' and never started the day without committing it to memory and praying that God would help him to put it into practice during that day. The inspiration of this habit must have encouraged hundreds of young people to start to hide the Scriptures in their hearts also.

Almost every weekend, Grandpa delivered the same talk in his staccato, military style. He had been a colonel in the army and had never forgotten it. The talk was entitled 'The sweet P's' and he delivered it with his white moustache bristling. 'When you read the Bible,' he would bark, 'you can't treat it as any ordinary book. It is God's word and God speaks through it to you as you read. So you start orff – (I'm not sure why he inserted the letter 'r' in the word 'off', but he always did) – you start orff by *Praying*. Then you read the *Portion* of the Bible for the day. Next you *Ponder* its meaning. Before you shut the book, you should identify a key phrase that sums up the meaning of what you have read. This you learn by heart and treat as your

Password for the day. Then go orff and put it into *Practice*.'

In our staff devotions one day we read of the third great Jewish festival recorded in the Bible, the Feast of Tabernacles. 'We celebrate the Passover at Eastertime. Why don't we make anything of the Feast of Tabernacles?' someone asked.

'It must be because the feast was essentially an open-air affair which fell into the calendar of events in mid-October. That may be well and good in the Middle East, but to build booths and sleep in the open in an English October you'd have to be orff your head,' Grandpa chuckled.

'So let's change the date,' I suggested. 'Let's celebrate the festival of Tabernacles in July.'

And that is what we did. Several hundred young people came for an eight-day open-air re-enactment of the ancient Jewish festival. The Green Hill, a shoulder of the North Downs adjacent to Hildenborough Hall, was covered with booths built from tree branches and bracken. Each night there was music and dancing by firelight, and each morning we read aloud from the Bible for two straight hours. The whole event was a fascinating experience and made the Bible live in a new way to all who took part.

The great thing about working at Hildenborough was the infinite scope it gave for creative worship. The place was alive with music and drama, all expressing the greatness of God. I wrote a musical for PACE to use in schools. Hundreds of guests passed through the place every week, people who needed feeding or a bed for the night. Each person gave us the opportunity to express worship to God through providing their needs. Every weekend we had two whole days and fifty-five acres to make the Bible live to a fresh group of young people, many of whom had never opened the book in their lives.

Joy and I lived close to Hildenborough Hall in an idyllic little house, mysteriously named Munda by the previous owners, who had spent much of their lives in Africa. We always wondered what 'Munda' meant, imagining something appropriate like 'little house in the woods'. Then one day an ex-missionary from Africa informed us that in the tongue of the people with whom she had worked it simply meant 'stomach'. While we were living in Munda, our three children, Esther, Daniel and Rebecca, were born. We appreciated the quietness of our secluded home and went there at the end of intensive weekends to collapse with a cup of coffee and the TV.

But just over the fields were Max and Sue with their three children. They lived a very different home life. Max was always building something. 'How do you like my latest creation?' He indicated a series of wooden posts linked with trelliswork. 'I call it "Wood Henge",' he told me proudly.

'I'm sure even the Druids would be impressed, but what exactly is it?'

'Can't you tell? It's a climbing-rose garden.'

Max and Sue were like that, always on the go. They had a huge vegetable garden and ate fresh produce, slugs and all. They kept lambs till they grew into sheep. Then they ate them. There were chickens and ducks. Sue made elderflower wine, which she insisted was non-alcoholic but which never failed to cheer up a dull dinner party! Her peanut butter was not smooth and creamy like our shop-bought variety. She used the whole nut, as far as I could discern, shell and all, so as not to miss any of the good nutrients! If there was any energy left over they would play tennis, or we would see them jogging down the lane past our home. When we spoke at meetings together, Max would always introduce us in the same way: 'We are cousins. God gives us our relatives, but thank goodness we can choose our friends!' There was a kind of friendly banter and rivalry that existed between us that made for many a good laugh.

So we were blessed with a wonderful family, good friends and a rewarding ministry. We were set for life with no cloud in the sky.

During those years I must have heard and delivered more talks than most preachers do in a lifetime. For the most part those talks are lost in the archives of my memory. One talk, however, is not forgotten, for it was to prove prophetic.

The theme of the weekend was 'Christian Warfare'. Ephesians 6 was the key passage from the Bible, for it lists a useful inventory of available hardware for the Christian's protection. I was the speaker.

'Now the shield is the symbol of faith. It was not a kind of inverted garbage-can lid which would have served merely to ward off darts and arrows like a perverted tennis racquet. But it was a big rectangle, something like a door bent in at the sides. Behind it, a man was totally shielded from any extraneous projectile which might happen his way.

'If a soldier needed a lesson on trusting his armour it would have been little good his staying home and polishing his shield. He might have measured its thickness and bolstered his courage with scientific calculations on its durability and density. Yet that would have done little to increase his faith in its protective qualities. He would never learn to trust his shield till he tried it. Let him walk out in front of a firing squad and let all Hell break loose on the other side of his shield. He might stagger home with his ears ringing. He might be upset to see his once shiny shield all dented and tarnished. Yet he would be assured that his shield was to be trusted. Such faith would give him the reckless, daring confidence that he would one day need in the face of the enemy.

'If you are ever to learn to have a faith in God which can act as your shield, then it's no good staying home studying theology and polishing up your Bible knowledge. Useful as those things may be, they are no substitute for standing in front of a spiritual firing squad, listening to all Hell breaking against the far side of your shield. Your ideas of God may look a little dented and tarnished as a result, but your faith will be real.'

It was stirring stuff! It must have been, because I still remember it. That is one of the perks of being a preacher. Your sermons make a deeper impression on you than on anyone else.

Someone raised a question:

'How can we put ourselves in a position where we can test out God's dependability?'

'We can't,' was my reply, 'for the Bible tells us not to put the Lord our God to the test. Jesus taught us to pray, "Lead us not into temptation." Yet he included a follow-up request just in case of trouble: "But deliver us from the evil one." In other words, if God should choose to allow us to be led into temptation despite our request that he should not do so, we would trust him to deliver us from the possible evil consequences of temptation. You see, while it may not be acceptable for us to put God to the test, there is nothing to prevent God from putting us to it. If you ask him to increase your faith, be warned! Keep your head low! For the next request not to be led into temptation is likely to get a negative response. But just remember this: if he should choose to lead you into temptation, then be assured that he can and will deliver you from the evil one. Your shield can take all that Hell has to throw at it, and proving that is the best and only way to increase your faith.'

I led the group in a prayer, challenging them to pray individually asking God to increase their faith. A terrible sense of hypocrisy came over me and I was shamed into meaning the prayer myself, personally.

'Amen!' I concluded, but that was only the beginning.

The firing squad was taking aim, and my faith was the target.

3

Green Faith

My mother was my greatest fan, and nothing I ever did was
less than the achievement of a genius, in her eyes at least.
My attempts at painting were on a level with those of
Rembrandt. My musical compositions challenged Mozart.
My athletic promise in the egg and spoon race fore-
shadowed an Olympic gold. I thank God for that kind of
devotion, which helped me through those awkward years
of adolescence when no one believed in me, least of all
myself.

On the day I was born, my mother, who made it a life
practice to read a passage of the Bible daily, read John the
Baptist's birth announcement. The angel Gabriel told
Zechariah that his son would be a preacher.

> *He will be great in the sight of the Lord . . . Many of the
> people of Israel will he bring back to the Lord their
> God. And he will go on before the Lord, in the spirit and
> power of Elijah, to turn the hearts of the fathers to their
> children and the disobedient to the wisdom of the right-
> eous – to make ready a people prepared for the Lord.*

'One day you'll be a preacher,' Mother assured me, long
before I even knew what a preacher was. I never had an

ambition to drive a fire engine or to be a policeman. I always had a sense of destiny that I would be a preacher. 'He will turn the hearts of the fathers to their children and the disobedient to the wisdom of the just.' I didn't know what that meant, but I knew I would do it!

My sister Jennifer and I attended Sunday School in a tiny gospel hall in the village of Hildenborough where we lived. Mother's maiden name was Sinclair, and her Scottish blood dictated that she send me to Sunday School dressed in a kilt, a matter of acute embarrassment to me as I was the only one wearing a skirt on the boys' side of the aisle. It was therefore necessary for me to prove my masculinity through worse behaviour than that of my fellow students.

One day Mr Lansdale, the teacher, produced a copy of Holman Hunt's famous painting of Jesus knocking at the door. We learned by heart the well-known verse from the book of Revelation which had inspired the artist: '*Here I am! I stand at the door and knock. If anyone hears my voice and opens the door, I will come in and eat with him, and he with me.*'

Mr Lansdale then taught us a new song.

Into my heart; into my heart;
Come into my heart, Lord Jesus.
Come in today. Come in to stay.
Come into my heart, Lord Jesus.

As Jen and I walked home up the tree-lined drive to Hildenborough Hall, Jen, a blunt ten-year-old, informed me that I was not a Christian because I had never asked Jesus to come into my heart. Being four years her junior, I assumed that she must be right, and readily desired to rectify my shortcoming.

'But what do I say?' I asked her.

Standing quietly at the foot of a huge tree with spongy bark, I repeated the words of the song we had learned at Sunday School: 'Into my heart; into my heart; come into my heart, Lord Jesus. Come in today. Come in to stay. Come into my heart, Lord Jesus.'

To this day that event stands out in my life as a significant milestone.

I recall a family outing when I was eight years old. We had persuaded a fisherman to take us all for a joy ride round Hestan Island on the Solway coast of Scotland. All was calm till we reached the seaward side. There, two currents conflicted and the waves stood up in protest. Doubtless there was no real danger, but at the time no such assurance was ours. Certain death seemed to stare us in the face, the extinction of the Rees family.

Rather like the apostle Paul in similar circumstances, I addressed the assembled company: 'You may all be in danger, but I am not.'

'Just how do you come to that conclusion?'

'Easy! You see, God has promised that I will be a preacher. I'm not one yet, but one day I will be. Till then I am safe! Stay close to me and you may also be saved.'

No wonder the precocious Joseph's family sent him off to Egypt when he made similar boasts. It was a wonder my family didn't throw me overboard. Maybe if they had, a whale would have swallowed me! Who knows?

Mid-life crisis is the time when you come to terms with the regrettable conclusions that your mother's exaggerated assessment of your abilities is not going to translate into the person you hoped to become. You are not going to be prime minister or president after all. It's the transition between childhood dreams and adult realities.

It may have been the onset of mid-life which started me questioning my mother's predictions. Perhaps this life-directing verse was nothing more than the doting optimism of a loving mother, and therefore the idea should be discarded along with thoughts of grandeur as a composer, artist or athlete.

All this may seem trivial or even amusing, but attached to this expectation of life was a bomb which was bound to explode sooner or later. My faith in God was intricately bound up in my expectation that he would make me a preacher. If what I had always understood as my God-ordained vocation was nothing more than Mother's wishful thinking, then maybe God didn't care what I did with my life after all. That is a very insecure feeling for one who has lived all his life with a very strong sense of calling.

The bomb's fuse was finally ignited by a seemingly unrelated incident.

Since we had taken on the work at Hildenborough Hall, Joy and I had been living in Munda, the bungalow at the foot of the driveway. It was a lovely home, but it isolated us from the real world beyond the fields and woodlands of Kent. Our children were now attending school, which demanded hours of driving them to and fro. We therefore had our eyes open for a house in one of the neighbouring villages.

Broughton Manor was built in the fifteenth century. King Henry VIII owned it for a while, maintaining it as a lodge for his expeditions to hunt wild boar on the North

Downs of Kent. The property has since passed through the custodianship (for one never really owns a property like that) of many commoners. Mr Roberts had lived there for some thirty years, but with the onset of years he was forced to put it on the market at a time when the value of large old houses was at rock bottom. King Henry never considered the prohibitive costs of central heating. But to the buyer in the twentieth century, that is a very important consideration. So when Mr Roberts had the property valued, he was amazed at how little it was worth.

When I saw it advertised, I too was amazed. I obtained details from the estate agent and made an appointment to view it.

Joy and I walked round the house like people in an exclusive jewellery store, dazzled by the magnificence of the display, awed by our own unworthiness to buy so much as one small trinket. Exposed timbers were everywhere. Inglenook fireplaces offered cosiness. A great hall, complete with minstrels' gallery, promised the ideal venue for entertaining. Twelve intriguing acres surrounded the house, with a lake, stream, waterfall, orchard, rose garden and paddock. It even had a small cottage situated in the grounds, which would have been ideal for accommodating Mother in her old age. There was an oast house and barn, ripe for conversion to further living accommodation. What a paradise for a growing family!

When one considered the finances of the thing there was nothing but encouragement. The oast barn could be sold off, with six acres. Once that sale was complete, the manor house and the cottage with the remaining acres would have cost us less than we anticipated realising from the sale of Munda. What an investment! What a home!

We hardly slept a wink that night as we thought about it. The only cloud on the horizon was what people would think of Justyn and Joy living in a manor house! Still, we could explain the 'good stewardship' to those who asked and leave the others to guess or criticise.

The next day was Saturday. Being in no rush to get to work, I sat in the lounge and leisurely read the passage from my Bible suggested by the study guide I was following for that day. My mind was only half on what I was reading because the other half was wandering round Broughton Manor.

Suddenly I was wide awake, my attention riveted to Deuteronomy 11. '*You shall teach them to your children, talking to them when you are sitting in your house*', (what other house could it be referring to but Broughton Manor!) '. . . *when you are walking by the way,*' (there was the lake, the orchard, the rose garden, the paddock) '. . . *and when you lie down and when you rise*' (there was the great vaulted ceiling in the master bedroom above a four-poster bed containing Joy and me and the three children as I read aloud from the Bible). '*You shall write them upon the door posts of your house and upon your gates*' (the crest on the wrought iron gates would be really enhanced by some Bible quotation or other). '*The Lord will drive out those nations before you*' (it was comforting to know that we could count on divine intervention in the negotiations to purchase; that should save us a few pounds). '*Every place on which the sole of your foot treads shall be yours*' (perhaps we shouldn't sell off the oast barn, after all).

'Hey! Joy! Come here and listen to this.' Joy came through from the kitchen, drying her hands as she looked over my shoulder.

'We must be careful not to read things into the Scriptures which were never intended to be there.' I hate it when Joy disagrees with me, especially when she is right.

'Yes, but the coincidence of this reading with our present interest in Broughton Manor is remarkable,' I protested. 'It isn't as though I had hunted for this passage. It just happens to be the portion of the Bible that is set for the day by this study guide.'

We prayed: 'O Lord, if this is your encouragement to go ahead with an offer, then please confirm it to us.'

There was nothing we could do to take the matter further, for the great British weekend paralysed activity. So we went for a walk around the outside of the six-foot brick walls which concealed the grounds of Broughton Manor. 'Every place on which the sole of your foot treads shall be yours.' Be sure we trod carefully. Joshua and his friends walking around the walls of Jericho had no greater sense of anticipation.

Now I like to think that I am more spiritually minded than Joy because I read the Bible in the morning, while she waits till evening before she reads her daily chapter. But in reality I see that it has much more to do with the nature of the housewife's lot. Little children rarely afford a young mother the luxury of a few peaceful minutes to herself for reading the Bible, or any other book for that matter, especially in the morning.

So that night, when the children were asleep and tucked up in bed and I was already drifting off into a sleepy no-man's-land, suddenly Joy sat bolt upright in bed.

'Jay!' (that's what she calls me when she's excited), 'Jay, look at this.'

I didn't look, but I listened. '*Go into the land which I*

*am giving you . . . Every place that the sole of your foot
shall tread upon I have given to you as I promised.'*

'Remarkable,' I said, rejoicing that now I had the
opportunity of appearing the cool one. 'That is the same
passage that I read this morning. I thought you were
following a different study guide than mine.'

'I am, and that is not the same passage you read from
Deuteronomy. This comes from Joshua 1 and is the featured
memory verse of the week.'

'Let me see,' I said, sitting up and losing my cool
composure.

Another sleepless night followed, and consequently the
Sunday morning service was a struggle for survival. But
you have never seen a more alert couple than were Joy and
I when the preacher read his text:

*These words which I command you this day shall be
upon your heart; you shall teach them diligently to your
children, you shall talk of them when you sit in your
house, and when you walk by the way, and when you lie
down and when you rise . . . And you shall write them on
the door posts of your house and on your gates . . . when
the Lord your God brings you into the land.*

It was a repeat neither of Joy's reading nor of mine. This
time it was from Deuteronomy 6. I never knew that the
Bible was so full of references to Broughton Manor!

Now I don't want to paint a picture of myself as a
complete idiot, so let me say that I had been raised on the
idea that, in the matter of decision-making, God was always
more anxious to guide us than we were to be guided.
Any decision should first be tested against the standards

of Scripture, then by seeking the wise counsel of Christian friends, and finally by reacting appropriately to the immediate circumstances of the decision.

The appropriate reaction to the immediate circumstances seemed obvious. Scripture appeared to be using a megaphone to direct us. That left us with the need to get the advice of Christian friends.

A chartered surveyor confirmed the soundness of the structure. There were no beetles or dry rot. 'It has stood for five hundred years, so it stands a good chance of surviving for your lifetime,' he reassured us.

Tim Giles, a chartered accountant friend, perused the figures and agreed the wisdom of the investment, 'if you don't mind cold winters, for I don't know how anyone could ever afford to heat it'. Then he strayed outside his specific field of accountancy and recounted to us the story of a Christian organisation whose accounts he kept, and who had felt a similar leading to purchase a particular property. They too had walked the perimeter fence, claiming the property in the Lord's name. At one point, however, because of some idiosyncrasy of the terrain, they had been forced to cut across a corner of the land. When eventually they did buy it, that corner had been removed from the sale to make way for a new road!

Even Joy's mother and father could see the potential of Broughton Manor, though they too warned us of the cold and the hard work to maintain it.

A row of green lights was before us. We made an offer. The agent was slow to present it to Mr Roberts. Days dragged by.

'Jay, I have discovered something very terrible,' Joy told me one lunchtime. 'Remember my friend, Christine?'

Christine was a friend who Joy was keen to introduce to Jesus. 'Well, apparently she is a close friend of the caretaker, Len Norris, who is currently living in the cottage of Broughton Manor. She told me today that he is planning to sit tight and never move out. Apparently he has a legal right to stay there as long as he chooses.'

'No, that is not correct,' I reassured her. 'It will be possible to move him out if he is no longer employed as the caretaker.'

'Yes, but even if that is so, we couldn't possibly evict him. How would we ever face Christine again?'

Which was more important to us, Christine's friendship and her becoming a Christian, or Broughton Manor? So we contacted the estate agent and withdrew our offer.

We would have been miserable except for the assurance that God himself had promised to 'drive out the inhabitants'. The same kind of confidence bolstered me up as that which I had experienced in the near-disastrous family outing in the fishing-boat trip round Hestan Island.

A month passed. Then, walking down the village high street, I encountered a face which looked vaguely familiar. I had just passed it when my subconscious memory solved the riddle.

'Hello, Len!' He swung round. It was the caretaker from Broughton Manor.

'Do you remember me?' I enquired. 'I was one of the people interested in buying your house.' He did remember. 'Has it sold yet?'

'Sold? No! Haven't you heard? The old man, Mr Roberts, died a couple of weeks back and so the sale has been delayed while the trustees of his will get things sorted out. The worst part of it all is that they have kicked me out and

I thought I was safe there as long as I wanted.'

I should have felt sorry for him, but all I could think was that the Lord had kept his promise and 'driven out the inhabitants of the land'. Now we were free to resubmit our offer, as there was no conflict of interests.

Our offer was accepted and I went off to Italy to participate in a two-week conference. When I returned, I discovered that our offer had been 'unaccepted'. A higher offer had been put in by somebody else while I was away.

'But my offer has been accepted,' I reminded the agent.

'There was no binding contract.'

It was as simple as that. There was no room for argument or further negotiation. The suggestion that our agreement might have been morally binding, even if it wasn't legally so, held no water. The other offer had been signed and sealed and now was legally binding. We had been gazumped.

But we still had the promises of God to reassure us, and we stubbornly hung on to them till our rival moved in.

We were baffled, disappointed and let down.

It was Christmas the following winter. Broughton Manor was fading but a question was still in the 'pending file' of our minds.

I was the speaker at a Christmas house party at Hildenborough Hall and resolved to lead a study on the doubts of Zechariah contrasted with the faith of Mary. Both had seen the angel. One had doubted, the other had believed the message. Zechariah, as a priest, should have known better! He treated the angel Gabriel much as Ebenezer Scrooge treated Marley's ghost. 'Humbug! How shall I know this is true?' He was struck dumb, for only a dummy would doubt God's word. I was fascinated by the thought that the angel left Mary with no room to doubt. Very graciously, he gave her the opportunity to check out the truth of what he had said. 'You are going to be the mother of the Son of God. No human husband will be needed for you to conceive, for the power of the Most High will overshadow you. If you want to check if these things are true, then go and visit your aunt, Elizabeth, the one who is barren and past the age for child-bearing. You will find that she too is in the family way.'

Unlike her Uncle Zechariah, Mary expressed no doubts. Yet she still checked out the detail of what she had been told. At the first opportunity, she packed her bags and set off to stay with her relatives in the south. There the two prophecies came together and confirmed one another. Aunt Elizabeth was indeed pregnant, as the angel had said she would be, and this impossibility reassured Mary of the certainty of the other impossibility. She, a virgin, would indeed give birth to a very special child.

Two unresolved questions from my mental 'pending file' jumped out on to my desk. God had promised through Mother's Bible reading that I would be a preacher who would 'bring many back to the Lord their God'. That was the very same prophecy that Zechariah had doubted, to his cost, when first the promise had been given. And God had also promised, through our own Bible readings, that we would 'possess' that patch of land, Broughton Manor. We had not reacted to either 'prophecy' with unbelief, as had Zechariah. Had we done so, we might have had cause to wonder if we had failed to enter because of unbelief. But we had never doubted. Were we misusing the Bible? If we were, then we were doing so for both prophecies. If we had misconstrued the Broughton Manor readings then maybe we had no grounds for pursuing the notion of my being a preacher, either.

What was I to do? Was there some way I could check one prophecy out against the other, as had Mary? I didn't mind too much about the house, but I cared very much about the calling to preach. If only we had been given that house then I might have been able to be more confident about my future as a preacher. I suffered from a terrible sense of inadequacy as a preacher as it was, and only Mother's prophecy made me persevere. To face reality was to wonder if we would be wiser to seek another career or way of serving God. But, in any case, I certainly didn't want to be like Zechariah, whose unbelief rendered him dumb.

I took the question to Fairlight beach, near Hastings. There I walked between the pounding surf and the crumbling white cliffs. There was no one but the seagulls to overhear me pouring out my heart to the Lord.

As the cliffs and the sea hemmed me in, so I was trapped between trusting God's promises that I would be a preacher, on the one hand, and the sense of guilt I felt for the presumption that I could ever be worthy to preach the gospel. The coincidence of our Bible readings and the availability of Broughton Manor had suggested to us that this was another promise of God to be trusted, yet we felt guilty for presuming to live in such a house. To desire Broughton Manor, or to cherish an ambition as to preach, was covetousness. On the other hand, to reject these 'promises' would be unbelief. I couldn't win.

Eventually I fell to my knees on a rock, and with the waves pounding at my heels and the seagulls screaming overhead, I committed the impasse to God.

As I walked back to the car it occurred to me that Mary took action. She didn't just wait and see. She went to visit Elizabeth. Right! I too would take action. I must presume that the promises were true and take steps to realise them.

That evening I wrote a letter to the new owner of Broughton Manor.

> Dear Sir,
> May I congratulate you on your new home.
> I hope you will forgive my writing to you in this way, but I too bid to purchase Broughton Manor. It occurs to me that just possibly you might not find the house to your liking, and if that should ever prove to be the case, then I should be most grateful if you would give me the possibility of buying it from you.
> Yours faithfully

Two weeks later the reply came.

> Dear Mr Rees,
> I am in receipt of your letter, for which I thank you.
> It is indeed strange that you should write, for I have come to the conclusion that Broughton Manor does not ideally suit my family's needs. I should therefore be glad to meet with you to discuss a possible sale.
> Yours sincerely,
> Martin Stevens

How foolish we had been even to wonder if God would keep his promises! With new confidence, we could renew negotiations for the property and push ahead with the conviction that God had indeed called me to preach the gospel. Wonderful! So faith was to triumph after all. The Bible was right:

If you assign your nuggets to the dust, your gold to the rocks in the ravines, then the Almighty will be your gold, the choicest silver for you. Surely then you will find delight in the Almighty and will lift up your face to God. You will pray to him, and he will hear you. What you decide on will be done, and light will shine on your ways.

We went to visit Mr Stevens in our future home. He had done some tasteful improvements which he proudly showed us. As we walked round the familiar building we sensed that every place we were treading upon God was giving us.

We sat down in the great hall. A blazing fire was burning in the inglenook fireplace under the minstrels' gallery.

Eventually the conversation came round to the vital question of money. 'How much were you thinking of asking?' I hazarded.

I nearly spat my coffee all over the beautiful Persian rug when he told me. He had doubled the price we had previously been willing to pay, yet was not planning to include the oast barn and the six-acre paddock in the sale.

I protested. He held firm.

Time proved his valuation reasonable, for it sold again, but not to me.

The new owner moved in, and my sense of calling as a preacher and security of purpose on God's earth began to move out.

4

Ten Green Bottles

'Justyn, I'm just calling you to let you know that Pop has been taken into hospital for observation. He had a funny turn this afternoon, so I called in the doctor who thought it wise to have him in for a day or two, so they can keep an eye on him.'

My mother-in-law's voice sounded reassuring, yet it was clear that all was not well.

Joy is a qualified nurse – a mixed blessing in the circumstances, for while she knew what to do in a crisis, she also knew too much for her own peace of mind. Her father's behaviour had been causing us all concern – loss of memory, dizzy spells, double vision, sudden flares of anger, and now this.

We went to visit him and were relieved to find him very much his usual self, if a little disgruntled at being in hospital instead of on his beloved farm.

'They think my heart is acting up again,' he told us.

'It's not his heart they should be looking at. It's his head that's wrong.' My mother-in-law's later diagnosis was very perceptive.

That weekend we jumped every time the phone rang, fearing bad news. Mercifully, I was not responsible for the teaching at Hildenborough Hall. Quintin Carr was on duty.

Young people just loved his speaking. He always treated them with respect and never spoke down to them or pretended he was trendy. 'I'm Grandpa,' he would introduce himself. 'I'm very, very old. I live at the bottom of the hill in a little wooden hut.' Then he'd add the line about the banana skin.

That particular weekend he poured out his soul, telling us of the love of God and the wonder of the Lord Jesus Christ. He urged us to holy living. 'Read the Bible every day. Follow the "sweet P's".' I must have heard him give that talk a hundred times, but that is the secret of godly living, so he kept at it.

Sunday afternoon he wished every guest goodbye, by name of course, then gave us a cheery wave as he set 'orff' to drive up to London to take part in a radio programme.

The telephone call we had dreaded came about ten that evening.

Joy saw the shock on my face as I turned from the phone.

'Dad?' she gasped.

'No. Grandpa.'

Hurrying back to his car from the studio, Quintin Carr had suffered his third heart attack and had collapsed and died all on his own in the London rain.

For hours we lay awake that night, caught in the upsurge of the currents of conflicting emotions. We were devastated by Grandpa's death. We were relieved that Joy's father was still with us. We felt guilty for feeling relief when Quintin was dead.

Following Quintin's cremation, his wife, Joyce, asked me if I would scatter his ashes. A small group of us huddled on the Green Hill. We recalled the past summer when we had held the Festival of Tabernacles on that same hillside and Grandpa's voice had filled the air with encouragement and laughter. Then brightly coloured flowers had turned the hillside from green to yellow. Now only husks remained.

I said my piece, fighting back the tears and trying to express so much in a sentence or two. The wind whipped the ashes away over the hill, and we headed for shelter.

Since my father had died six years previously, Grandpa had been one of two men I had leaned on for guidance and counsel. The other was in hospital with what soon was officially diagnosed as a brain tumour.

'Mrs Stordy,' the doctor had told my mother-in-law, 'I have something very serious to discuss with you.'

Isobel Stordy was courageous. Looking him in the eye, she told him that she and her husband had lived all their lives in anticipation of seeing the Lord Jesus Christ face to face, so she feared nothing he might have to tell her.

They took him into the Brook Hospital to see what could be done by surgery. He went in a seemingly healthy man. A week later he was released, disorientated, unable to utter anything but a confused jumble of sounds. The tumour was all through his brain and there was nothing anyone could do for him. They gave him six months at the most.

Over the winter he regained the ability to make himself understood to a limited extent, though his speech was never free of confusion and muddled sounds. However, on one occasion when the family were gathered, he surprised us all. At the end of the day, around the time when his habit had always been to lead us in family prayers, he signed that he wanted to pray. We were a little dubious, for it was occasions like this which accentuated his illness and caused embarrassment and grief. But he would not be refused. The prayer he offered was word perfect – no confusion, no strange sounds, just the prayer of a humble man who knows his God as a close friend.

Could it be that prayer is something which is offered from the soul rather than from the mind? His heart was right before God, though his brain was diseased. A year later this observation would return to encourage me.

Many friends called by to pray for him. Most prayed for a sense of God's presence to be with him and peace for all the family.

One person came and, with apostolic fervour, urged on all of us the duty of a faith which could move mountains, raise the dead and most certainly heal the sick. 'All you have to do is believe. Don't you want to see him healed? Then trust God for a miracle. "*The prayer offered in faith will make the sick person well.*" '

After our well-meaning friend had left, it was apparent we were all shaken. Isobel made a cup of tea.

'Why was that so disturbing?' Somebody raised the question we were all turning over.

Quietly, the person with the most to lose put us all wise. 'There is a world of difference between "trusting God for a miracle" and "trusting God". The first kind of faith is demanding, but the second is grateful and full of peace. God alone is qualified to make life-and-death decisions, and he is able to do whatever his perfect love tells him is for the very best. We can rest easy in the assurance that Pop's life is in the hands of one who loves him far more than any of us.'

The day came when it was apparent that the end was very near. Stephen, Joy's youngest brother, arrived from Africa, where he was on missionary service. He got home just in time to be recognised by his father before he slipped into unconsciousness.

We all sat with him as he died. How awesome it is to see a loved one off to Glory. One moment he was there with us, alive and breathing. We could touch him and talk to him. Then he was gone, and all we had left was a body. He was not there any more. He was with Jesus. We sat there gaping as the doors of death closed behind him. Heaven seemed very close.

Two much-loved and admired men were gone in the course of five months. Both were leading members of the Council of Management for Hildenborough Hall. It was vital to find a senior man of wisdom and experience to take their place.

'How about Walter Moss?' Max suggested at a Council meeting. Walter was recently retired. He lived nearby with his wife, Alys. Together, they had frequently hosted Hildenborough events, so he was an ideal choice.

Our unanimous agreement was matched by Walter's own enthusiasm. The ranks were closed where previous warriors had fallen.

As is often the way, this period of trauma was balanced with tremendous joy in the work we were doing. Max and PACE were constantly out on the road, spending days and sometimes whole weeks in schools, sharing their faith. Sometimes I went with them. One such visit from that period sticks out in my memory.

The school had the usual prison-like appearance, but this one had a prison-like atmosphere to match. Hatred glared from all around. This west London school had all the seeds of the race riots which were soon to erupt into violence. The staff hated the kids and the feelings were mutual. Everyone mistrusted everyone.

One small group of young students contrasted like roses on a dung heap. They met each morning before classes to pray, just six insignificant kids out of fifteen hundred. They were looking to God for a miracle. They wanted him to change their world.

When the Hildenborough team, PACE, arrived to spend the whole week, we were greeted with hostile indifference. Lepers might have received a warmer welcome. Every morning, PACE did their musical thing at the assembly. Then we would split up and go in pairs to different social studies and religious education classes, as we were invited. Our arrival in each class resembled the emergence of the proverbial maggot from the proverbial cheese.

If I had asked whether apathy or ignorance was the greater problem in the school, doubtless I would have received the classic response: 'I don't know and I don't care.'

I tried the usual approaches, but discussion was not forthcoming, doubtless the fault of both ignorance and apathy. So halfway through the week I changed tack. Entering a class and encountering the usual non-response, I asked them, 'Do you know what I would love to see in this school?' (No reply, of course.) 'I would like to see a community of people, staff and students, who respect each other, trust each other, and, above all, love each other.' A reaction at last! They laughed in my face. Yet on the faces of a couple of students I caught a flicker of something else, a faraway longing, the vague recollection of a dream.

I repeated it in class after class, telling them how Jesus

had always stuck out from the crowd in the way he treated people. He respected the outcasts, spoke to the Samaritan woman, touched the leper, befriended the unpopular and lovingly forgave even those who crucified him. When I told them that Jesus respected and loved them too, many looked wistful. But each time I came back to the idea of people loving and respecting each other in that school, they always laughed.

Friday came at last, and we invited any who were interested to come back that evening for a concert which PACE would present in the gymnasium. The concert, we warned them, would include an explanation of what it meant to be a real Christian and to follow Jesus Christ. Optimistically we set out fifty chairs, but we should have remembered those few kids praying each morning. Four hundred came! At the end of the evening, ninety rose to their feet in front of their cynical fellows to declare their intention to follow Jesus Christ.

Meanwhile, back at base, it was also harvest time.

Each weekend was jammed to capacity with young people earnestly seeking God, and better yet, finding him.

Saturday evenings were open to non-residents. We invited celebrities to come to share their faith with the visitors. Cliff Richard sang his faith. Malcolm Muggeridge philosophised it. Sir Norman Anderson reasoned it as in a court of law. Brother Andrew smuggled it. Graham Kerr served it up as a gourmet's delight. Graham Kendrick sang it for Jesus, for he hadn't thought of marching at that time. Everyone lapped it up, each according to his taste and personality. The result was dozens finding encouragement or first-time faith.

So great were the numbers attending that we were faced with the necessity to plan for expansion. Elaborate and expensive plans were drawn up and approved.

It was exciting to be at the helm of so flourishing an enterprise. Maybe Mother was not so wrong in her predictions, for many were indeed turning to God through my preaching. There was no time to consider Broughton Manor and the unsolved questions attached to it. It was a matter of getting on with what was there in front of our noses to be done.

With Walter Moss installed on the Council of Management, and the plans for expansion agreed, I decided to take the opportunity of getting away for a week's break. I badly wanted to gather my wits, which had been somewhat scattered by the events of the preceding few months, and I needed to spend time seeking God and his refreshment.

So I headed north to Scotland and then to the west coast. There was room to breathe and wilderness where one could walk and talk with the Lord for hours on end with no risk of bumping into another human being or of being overheard.

For three days I wandered over the hills and along the seashore, talking over the hurts I had felt over the deaths of those I had loved. I raised the matter of the uncertainty I had been feeling over the Broughton Manor affair and the consequent question-mark that had been placed over my determination to preach the gospel. I recalled my walk along the beach at Fairlight, four months previously. The pounding of the west-coast rollers on those steep Scottish rocks reminded me of the decision I had made to roll over the impasse to his broad shoulders. I was grateful for all that God was doing at Hildenborough and his mercy in allowing me the privilege of having a ringside seat to witness his faithfulness.

Feeling somewhat refreshed and with a desire to make contact with home, I headed into civilisation, to Oban, to find a telephone. What a lovely town, especially if you get there before or after the tourist rush. I located a phone on the dock but resolved to pay tribute to my Scottish environment by waiting till after six o'clock, when the cheap rates would be in force. There was a fish and chip shop open, so I bought a newspaper full of calories and settled on a bench to watch a fishing boat unload its day's catch. The seals poked up their snouts all around, looking for scraps, and the gulls swooped, hoping to cheat the seals. The sunlight sparkled on the water, and the dying day rejoiced in the goodness of its Creator.

At length, it was time to make the call. Joy sounded strained. It was she who needed the break more than I, for it was her father who had just died. But she couldn't leave the children.

'Jay, I have some rather sad news for you,' she shared at length.

I took a deep breath. Not more bad news.

'Walter Moss has just died of a heart attack.'

So I drove home, six hundred miles to wonder what in the world was going on. I was shaken. Was God trying to tell us something, or was the Devil trying to put a stop to the work?

Walter's funeral was held in an ancient village church. Plaques in remembrance of the dead lined the walls, and tombstones paved the floor. The vicar read the Scripture in a sad voice.

My days are swifter than a weaver's shuttle, and they come to an end without hope. Remember, O God, that my life is but a breath; as a cloud vanishes and is gone, so he who goes down to the grave does not return. He will never come to his house again; his place will know him no more.

As the eulogies continued I looked up the passage in the pew Bible and found it in the book of Job. The verse that followed struck a chord in my heart:

Therefore I will not keep silent; I will speak out in the anguish of my spirit, I will complain in the bitterness of my soul.

What in the world was God doing? Three deaths of three key people on the Hildenborough Council of Management, all within six months of each other. That was a lot to accept. Was I to take it lying down or should I lodge some kind of protest?

We had to elect a new chairman at the next Council meeting. It was eerie to see those three empty chairs. Nigel Cooke was recognised as the 'oldest surviving member' so he took over what was presenting itself as a very hot seat indeed. Who would be next? Nobody asked, but everyone wondered.

We held a combined meeting with the Hildenborough Trustees, a kind of 'House of Lords' or 'Senate'. It was made up of long-standing supporters of the work, men and women of wisdom but limited time, among them two bishops of the Church of England, Maurice Wood and John

Taylor, Bishops of Norwich and St Albans.

In so august and theological a setting, it was Max who raised the question I had been turning over in my mind during my drive back from Scotland.

'How should we view these events? Should we consider ourselves to be under the attack of Satan, in which case we should stand firm and fight? Or could it be that God himself is trying to communicate something to us, in which case we had better listen fast before we are all dead?'

John Taylor put us on the right track. 'Our responsibility as a Council is to make wise decisions based on the data available to us; in short, to manage this work. If we speculate about things we neither understand nor know anything about, then we will be in danger of failing in our God-given mandate to manage. We must ask God for wisdom, and trust him thereby to enable us to make wise choices. If we should still make decisions which time may show to have been wrong because of factors of which we are currently ignorant, then we must trust the Lord to overrule. But right now there are wise decisions to be made.' I guess they don't make you a bishop just for your ability to play croquet!

One of the 'wise decisions' which were reached that day was to give Joy and me a sabbatical rest. It had been back in the winter when we had first started to consider the possibility of our taking a prolonged break. We had been working at Hildenborough for coming up to seven years, and the recent months had taken their toll. I was grateful for the thought of three months away, particularly because I recognised Joy's need of a change following her father's death.

So, a few weeks later, we handed everything over to

Max, ably assisted by Felicity Lane in the office, and left Hildenborough in their very capable hands. What wonderful friends the Sinclairs were. You can take almost any amount of difficulty if there is someone to share it with. It was good to be able to go away with the easy feeling that everything was well taken care of. Three months stretched ahead and seemed like eternity.

We had been offered the use of a farmhouse in Northumberland if ever we had the time for a break. This was undoubtedly the time to take up the offer. I wanted to write a book. Esther wanted to be on a farm where there would be plenty of animals, and Dan wanted the sea to be nearby. Becky just wanted us all to be home, no matter where home might be located, and Joy wanted peace and quiet.

When you go to a place for the first time you are never quite sure what you are getting into. With some apprehension we drove out of Berwick on the road to Norham. There was the farm on the right, a huge old stone building set well back from the road amid meadows and trees. Heaven!

We found the key, as directed, under a brick in the back yard, by the dustbins. Cautiously we pushed open the door, feeling like intruders. A real farmhouse kitchen welcomed us, complete with Aga. Joy was in her element. The children disappeared. They always do when the car needs unpacking. We could hear them running about upstairs. Then all was quiet.

'Mum! Dad!' They burst in upon our peaceful cup of coffee. 'We have found Narnia! Come and see, oh please come now.' So we joined them exploring a labyrinth of hidden staircases and secret rooms behind wardrobes. The garden was alive with rabbits nibbling the grass and the fields were dotted with young lambs.

To get milk we had to take a tin churn down to the farm. Out it came, all frothy and creamy. For townies like us, it was enchanting.

That evening we went for a long walk over the fields and discovered a river, the Tweed, which formed one boundary to the farm. Dan resolved to make a raft and to float down to the sea.

Next morning we woke to find the sun streaming in through our window. Peace! No pressure to get up, no conference to cater for, no missions to plan, no staff to organise, no books to balance, nothing but a whole new area of the country to explore.

We set out for the village of Norham on our bicycles. There was a real castle standing proud above the river. The occupants must have been very careless, for, to the children's great delight, they each discovered treasure hidden in crevices around the crumbling walls. However did those ancient Britons have coins minted in the twentieth century? The children may have wondered, but the lady in the village shop never raised an eyebrow when presented with ancient treasure in exchange for ice creams and sweets.

In so idyllic an environment it was not surprising that the inspiration for my book came readily to mind. Next day I got cracking, and within three days we were settled into a happy routine. Every morning I would write and in the afternoons we would go off to seek adventure.

The traumas of the preceding few months were receding. Perspectives were being restored. We were having a family time such as we had never enjoyed before because of the constant intrusion of the conference centre. The future was full of hope.

On the fifth evening we were there, the phone rang. I jumped. It was the first time it had rung since we had arrived. I hate the telephone at the best of times, but at least this call couldn't possibly be for us, for no one knew our number. I hesitated, but then decided to answer just in case.

'Sue, how lovely to hear you!' It was Max's wife. 'How did you track us down?'

'I'm afraid I have some rather bad news.' I froze. This couldn't be happening. 'We had an accident this morning while driving home from visiting a friend in Devon.'

'Was anyone hurt?'

'Yes, Max was, but the rest of us are OK.'

'How badly is Max hurt?'

'I'm afraid he has broken his neck and is completely paralysed.'

We were just clearing away the supper things at the time and Becky was getting ready for bed. 'Come on,' I said, when they all knew as much as I. 'Let's pack.'

Within the hour we were heading south to Exeter where Max was in hospital. We drove much of the night and arrived at breakfast time.

Max looked awful, face drawn with pain and his head seemingly clamped by what looked like tongs. Joy's professional nurse's composure let her down and I pasted on what I determined to be a smile. It didn't work.

'What is the prognosis?' I asked Sue when we were out of earshot.

'It's too early to be sure about anything yet,' she shared.

'They are not even sure that he'll make it at all. But it seems certain that even if he does he will never be able to walk again.'

She was brave, never shedding a tear that I saw.

And so we headed back to Hildenborough, weeks ahead of schedule. It would be strange to be there without Max. How good it would have been to be able to talk the matter over with Grandpa, or Joy's father, or even Walter Moss. But they were all gone, and now Max was out of the picture too. At least he was not dead.

Within hours we had forgotten that we had even been away. The many demands of the centre pressed in. The chef came to me apologising for coming at a time like that, but it seemed that the Lord had told him that he was to leave immediately. I told him that it was a pity that the Lord had not seen fit to vouchsafe to him that directive before he had signed a contract which committed him to give three months' notice. He stayed!

Next in line was the housekeeper, whose health problems forced her to give three months' notice.

Then the water supply gave up the ghost the very same evening that a hundred Germans arrived, direct from the fatherland. We issued them each with a milk bottle full of water to clean their teeth, then pointed to the swimming pool. Two days and half a mile of thick black hose later, we did our ablutions.

Advertisements for chefs and housekeepers bore no fruit. At least there was Felicity, holding the fort in the office. The summer wore on. We paid various visits to Max, first in Exeter, then at Stoke Mandeville Hospital. He was a radiant example of how a Christian in those circumstances ought to act. The man in the next bed was paralysed from the waist down, so still had the use of his upper body. He radiated resentment. The doctors were incompetent for failing to cure him. The nurses were inattentive. God was supremely responsible for having totally wrecked his life, which had been going very nicely thank you till the Almighty decided to get involved. Max was intolerable because in spite of being in a worse predicament, he had the audacity to be cheerful and even grateful!

'Jay Bird,' said Sue, perverting my nickname one day while we were visiting, 'I want your advice. On the day after the accident I read a very relevant verse in my *Daily Light*.' (The *Daily Light* is a little book of selected readings from the Bible dated for each day of the year.) '*Is any among you sick? Let him call for the elders of the church, and let them pray over him, anointing him with oil in the name of the Lord; and the prayer of faith will save the sick man, and the Lord will raise him up.*'

'Max and I have been talking it over and we wondered if we shouldn't call for the elders. What do you think?'

I thought that if it was there in the Bible, then they should act accordingly, especially in view of the unmistakable coincidence of that passage being Sue's reading the very day after the accident. Coincidental readings seemed to be frequent in those days! But this one, at least, was not out of context.

I helped them compile a list of people they would consider to be 'Elders'. This was no easy task considering that the three most obvious choices were freshly in their graves. But we completed the list. Edward Smith was a long-time friend and recognised man of prayer. Marcus Collins was a lay reader from St Nicholas Church, where we all attended, and so was James Jones, as well as being a frequent speaker at Hildenborough.

The date they set was for three weeks' time, and everyone agreed to be there. Then they added one extra name to the list, mine. I didn't want to rock the boat, so I kept from them the fact that I was scheduled to be in Italy running a conference on the date they had all agreed. Yet nothing would prevent me from being there.

We drove out to Italy as a family. Running Hildenborough did have its advantages and certainly never lacked variety. I booked a flight home for the day of the Elders' prayer gathering, with a return for the following day. The conference would get by without me for thirty-six hours.

The Dolomite mountains in northern Italy are well worth the visit. Jagged peaks stab the sky from lush green valleys. Little hotels and restaurants nestle in forgotten hamlets. And it was in one of these that we stayed with our seventy guests. We had imported from England a very special guest speaker, Dr Alan Redpath. 'Uncle Alan', as we always called him, seemed to pop up in so many places and at so many vital times in our lives.

It was good to have such a man of God with us for that retreat. We stole him and Marjorie his wife from the rest of the party one day and set off up a chair lift in the hope of finding an interesting place for lunch. The man at the top, who spoke no English, responded to our hungry gesticulations by pointing along a path. We set off confidently. The path dwindled to a ledge. Uncle Alan got vertigo and there we stuck. I went ahead and found that the restaurant was just around the corner. So, bravely, with eyes closed and teeth clenched, Uncle Alan proceeded. Our efforts were barely rewarded, for the restaurant offered scant fare. Italian menus meant nothing to any of us. English meant even less to the waiter. So we pointed into our mouths and chewed and then mimed a drink. Rubbery cheese and stale bread was the response, but protest was useless. The coffee was acceptable.

'Tell me, Uncle Alan', I asked at length. 'How do you account for your close friendship with God? You seem to be so intimate, and when you speak it is like hearing from Heaven direct.'

He brushed it aside to begin with. 'Things aren't always what they seem,' he tried. But I persisted.

'If I had my life again I would take more time to pray. That is the simple answer. The secret is in relying on the Lord totally. While I was pastor of a big church in Chicago I was very busy in the Lord's service, but I had so little time for Jesus himself. Then a few years ago I had a stroke and I thought I'd never preach again. I found that the only thing I could do was pray. That was the greatest discovery of my life! If only I had made that discovery years sooner.'

'Does one have to wait till one is as old and decrepit as you to make that discovery?' I asked cheekily.

With a twinkle in his eye he assured me that I need wait no longer.

The day for the prayer gathering dawned bright. Such were the wonders of twentieth-century transportation that it was possible for me to wake up in a remote hamlet in Italy and have time to be in London for an afternoon appointment. Julius Caesar would have loved it.

I got up extra early so I would have time to pray and to prepare myself for the specific prayer we were meeting to offer that afternoon. I went out for a walk and climbed up high into the mountains. By and by I came upon a meadow full of flowers and fragrance. Here, I threw myself down and prayed in earnest that God would heal Max and enable him to climb up to that same place one day to enjoy its magnificence. I recalled reading *Heidi* aloud to my children, the moving story of the little girl whose courage and faith restored to her friend the ability to walk. It all happened on just such a mountain as the one on which I was sitting.

Then I returned to the valley below to take the bus to the airport. 'We'll be praying for you,' called a couple of conference members. 'What time will you be meeting with the Elders at the hospital?' I told them. 'We will meet to pray here at that same time.'

There was not a moment of peace till I settled into my window seat on the plane. I pulled out of my carry-on bag my own copy of the *Daily Light*. I turned to that day's dated reading, August 17th, and read the verses selected. It hit me between the eyes: 'Is any among you sick? Let him call for the elders . . .' The same words Sue had read the day after the accident which had prompted the very prayer gathering I was travelling to attend. Another amazing coincidence of Scripture! My worshipping spirit marvelled and my questioning mind remembered Broughton Manor. Perhaps it wasn't such a coincidence after all. Perhaps the *Daily Light* often repeated that verse from James 5. It probably cropped up every week! So I flipped to the index at the back to see how often that reference recurred. My cynicism received a slap in the face. It was only included twice. August 17th and July 23rd, the day of Max's accident. The book dropped open at the fly leaf. 'To Justyn and Joy.

May the Lord richly bless your marriage together. With much love, Uncle Alan and Auntie Marjorie.' The Redpaths had given us this book as a wedding present.

'Does one have to wait till one is as old and decrepit as you to make that discovery?' I had asked him only yesterday. I read on in James 5. 'The prayer of a righteous man has great power in its effects . . .' 'If I had my life again I would take more time to pray. That is the simple answer.' Alan Redpath was indeed 'a righteous man'. How I would love to be a man of prayer like him. 'O God, teach me to pray like that,' I breathed silently.

The longer the journey, the greater your expectations of your arrival. As I approached Stoke Mandeville my expectations were never higher. Certainly I had come a long way, but much more importantly I had received what must surely be the reassurance of the Lord that the trip would not be in vain. Then there was the knowledge that people all over the world were praying for Max at that very time. A crowd was meeting in the chapel at Hildenborough, and our conference members were meeting in northern Italy led by Alan Redpath, 'a righteous man' whose praying would have 'great power in its effects'. Many others knew that this special prayer was taking place and had promised to pause from whatever they were doing to pray at that very time. Surely God could not ignore so much prayer from so many righteous men.

Sue also had spotted the *Daily Light* reading and was full of enthusiasm. The other elders were more reserved as we gathered in the hospital chapel before going in to see Max. We shared with one another what we each had on our own heart to ask God to do for Max. I was in no doubt what

I wanted – an immediate miracle of healing. I hated to see him in such discomfort and I badly needed his help with the running of the centre. Then there were all the promises of Scripture to lead me to this obvious conclusion that complete and immediate healing was what I should ask for. That was what God was planning to do. We prayed and then went to find Max.

They had managed to arrange for the use of a small side room for the prayer, and so we had privacy. Max was quiet and subdued. If there was a lot riding on the outcome of this prayer session for me then there was much more for Max.

We managed a few cracks to ease the tension. He managed a weak grin. Then we got down to business. At Hildenborough, they prayed with fervour. In Italy, Alan Redpath and company prayed. All over the country, cars pulled over to the roadside and paused to pray, housewives closed their eyes at the sink, commuters shut out the noise of the train for a few seconds, teenagers put aside their homework. We all prayed to the God who promised to answer prayer. James Jones took a flask of oil and poured a few drops on to Max's scrawny neck and gently rubbed it in. We prayed some more. I kept my eyes open because I had never seen a miracle before and I sure wasn't going to miss this one.

Nothing happened. Nothing at all!

No one seemed surprised or even disappointed. Max was wheeled back into the main ward and we all stood round for a few minutes making polite conversation. Then we left.

As we drove home together: 'Well, that was tremendous, wasn't it?'

'Yes. Isn't Max's courage an inspiration?'

'And Sue's, too. What a courageous woman!'

'It was so right to go and anoint him with oil. Did you read the *Daily Light* this morning?'

'You are awfully quiet, Justyn. Guess you must be tired after the trip from Italy. Are you OK?'

'No, I am not OK. We went there today to pray that God would heal Max, and we had every reason to expect him to do so. And he didn't.'

'Oh yes, but sometimes these things take time. We mustn't rush God, you know. Maybe he doesn't plan to heal him at all. It would be a bad mistake to presume to know the mind of God.'

'Fiddlesticks!' I thought. 'That's a cop-out if ever there was one.' Out loud, I said, 'It's all very well for you all, but Max is my friend, and anyway, I badly need him back to help me run Hildenborough. For you, your responsibility is over, but mine is only just beginning.'

Before my plane took off next day, I made a call from the airport to ask Sue how Max had fared overnight. Perhaps he had made a dramatic improvement. In fact he had passed one of the worst nights since the accident and had nearly died from an asthmatic attack.

'We were all praying. How did it go?' everyone asked eagerly when I arrived back in Italy.

'It nearly killed him,' I told them bitterly.

5

Great Expectations

'Justyn, I feel compelled by the Lord to tell you what is on my heart.'

I mentally ducked. When you are in leadership you are inevitably the 'Aunt Sally' of people's criticism. When that criticism arrives, confirmed supposedly by the very signature of God, then you are in real trouble, for who can argue?

Felicity, the office administrator, had a big heart. Consequently, she had developed a deep concern for the wellbeing of the staff. She was what the character analysts call 'a people-oriented person', while I have always been 'task-oriented'. She orientated her thinking around the 'process', while my main concern was the 'product'. I am told that every organisation feels a tension between those two opposites.

'You are expecting too much of us all. I don't mind personally, but I don't feel it's fair on the newer members of staff.' Every hardship inflicted on the community by the worsening staff situation was the fault of management. I was the management. All others who might have been accused of being management were either in Heaven or in hospital, and were, therefore, unavailable.

Felicity was right. We were expecting too much of the

staff. But then I had the sole responsibility to keep the place ticking. Every day there were guests arriving for the programme we had been advertising for the previous six months. They had saved up their hard-earned cash and now here they were, eager with expectation. They needed spiritual help and counsel. This was their week's holiday or their weekend break. I couldn't disappoint them. But that was the 'task', my orientation. Staffing shortages were a part of the 'process', Felicity's orientation.

The situation was aggravated by the launching of a new scheme to make Hildenborough self-sufficient foodwise. The fifty acres which surrounded the centre were being developed to become a farm. David Calcott, a most excellent and experienced man, was in charge of the project, but it still took time. The kitchen department didn't take kindly to vegetables arriving still infested with caterpillars. The frozen variety came ready washed and wrapped in polythene. David's did not. Frozen chickens had no feathers or guts. David's had both. All these things took some readjustments.

Then there was the expansion programme which was being launched. That required hours of time with architects and builders. And there was the money to pay for it all. Someone had to ask for it and to write thank-you letters to the thousands of people who gave so sacrificially. One lady sent a large sum with a note enclosed: 'I was going to have central heating installed in my home but decided to send you the money instead.' Of course, I could send out standard thank-you letters. But each gift was a non-standard self-sacrifice and demanded genuine gratitude. Living at the receiving end of constant generosity is a very humbling experience, and also a very exhausting one. The thing I found so taxing was the feeling of guilt I experienced from the knowledge that every gift was an individual expression of love and support, yet I hardly had the time to sign the printed thank-you letter we sent back in response. Was it not hypocrisy to thus pretend our gratitude?

So Felicity had a point. I don't mind unjustified complaints, but the truth requires readjustments, and that takes time, and time was in short supply.

The housekeeper had left and the chef's three months were up. But the house still needed cleaning and dozens of hungry mouths turned up for meals three times a day. What were we to do? We had been advertising all summer, had written numerous letters to supporters, had offered bribes and incentives, both temporal and eternal, but had turned up no one to plug the gaps. It goes without saying that we had been praying, but on this occasion it seemed that even the Lord could find no one to help us.

Now Felicity wanted *me* to do something about it.

My response to her request was not that of a fine Christian leader. 'Task' and 'people' orientations clashed once again.

Yet something did have to be done. The house did have to be cleaned and the food did have to be put on the tables. That evening, as I was sitting in our nice clean home eating my delicious supper, it occurred to me that the one responsible for such provision might be the solution to Felicity's 'What are you going to do about it?'

Well, Joy couldn't possibly run both our own home and the conference centre at the same time, so we moved out of Munda and into a small apartment in Hildenborough Hall. I don't know how she did it, but she managed to care for three children and combine the roles of caterer and housekeeper, previously two full-time jobs.

That problem was solved. Felicity was happy. But Joy was stretched.

PACE, our roving band, had lost Max, their leader. I could hardly ask Joy to take that on as well, so I did it.

Then there was the new autumn season of weekends starting up, with no chaplain and no Max. It therefore fell to me to organise them, host them, speak at them. And all that took time.

I had no time. I could do nothing properly, for preparation had become a luxury I could ill afford. Consequently, I was failing in every aspect of my responsibilities, and the knowledge of that failure, together with a little help from Felicity, laid a crushing weight of guilt on me. The last thing I wanted to hear was a catalogue of my failures, but I heard it just the same. Inwardly I agreed but outwardly I gave my critics as good as I got.

'Do you know,' Felicity retorted on one occasion, 'God has laid on my heart that one day you will be a much used preacher, but I feel he is going to break you first.' That did not go with a swing. However much I might like the idea of being a preacher, the idea of being broken was unattractive.

Nevertheless, a sense of fatalism crept over me. What was written was written, and if Felicity and my mother were right then there was brokenness ahead, and that sounded painful. If they were wrong, then my dreams were broken anyway.

Occasionally I would hear cliques of the staff holding clandestine prayer meetings. It irritated me to realise that I was often the object of their prayers. I was the one who was the leader and should be the one praying for them. They were upsetting the balance and structure of things!

* * *

Yet there was much to be encouraged about. Max was making progress. It had started out as a tingling sensation in the tips of his fingers, but was now becoming small movements. Every day seemed to bring improvement. Perhaps he would walk after all.

Hildenborough Hall was packed every weekend. The Saturday evening events were particularly popular and attracted hundreds from all over the south-east of England. At the close of each programme I rounded off with an invitation to turn in faith to God and become a Christian. Dozens did.

But all these crowds of people added pressure to the team working behind the scenes. One of Felicity's big complaints was that the staff accommodation was inadequate. Well, phase one of the expansion programme would take care of that by providing a new staff home. Instead of building, we had decided to look for a suitable house close by Hildenborough Hall. This would offer the added bonus of giving staff members the sense of going home at night rather than always living 'over the shop'.

When our next-door neighbour decided to put his farmhouse up for sale, it seemed too coincidental to be anything other than God's provision. The bonus was that seventeen acres, some farm buildings and a dilapidated cottage went with the house. David Calcott's eyes lit up; just what he needed for the agricultural project. Everyone was very excited about Oakley Farm.

The money was arriving daily but thus far amounted to little more than a good down payment. A very important decision needed to be made. Should we wait till we had all the money in hand before making a definite offer to purchase, or should we move ahead 'in faith'? Having recently lost Broughton Manor to caution, I was inclined to push ahead. On the other hand, I hated the idea of committing ourselves to something we might not be able to pay for.

'It is all a matter of faith. Move forward in confidence that the Lord will supply all our needs.'

'That's right. If we wait till we have all the money in hand, then where will be the need to trust God? If we want to express faith then we must be prepared to take risks, to live dangerously.'

'But couldn't we trust God to provide our needs before we make the offer? Would that be any less an expression of faith? After all, we would then be trusting God to keep anyone else from buying Oakley Farm, as well as trusting him to provide the money to pay for it.'

'No. We must go out on a limb. Unless we are making ourselves vulnerable by taking a risk, we are not exercising faith.'

'But it would be taking a risk if we waited for the money, confident that God would hold the farm for us. By pushing ahead we might be accused of not "waiting on the Lord".'

'If "waiting on the Lord" meant doing nothing till God has "provided", then Noah would never have built the ark, Abraham would still be in Ur of the Chaldeans and David would never have killed Goliath.'

So the discussion waged on and on. Both sides were convincing. *Faith* was the prime requirement for either option. There was no escaping the need to trust God no matter which route we decided to follow. I sensed everyone looking to me to 'lead them out in faith'. Felicity was urging me to give a higher priority to the staff needs, so I must not risk disappointing her. Then there was the Broughton Manor saga, which seemed to demonstrate that 'waiting on God's provision' did not always pay off. But possibly the greatest factor in the equation was the suggestion that to hesitate was not to trust God. I must prove to myself and to others that I really do trust God.

So we made our offer. The offer was accepted. A contract was signed. Everyone was happy. We were committed to purchase Oakley Farm.

Every morning at the staff coffee break we made it our custom to spend time sharing information and then praying together. Every day we had an update from the book-keeper on the progress of the extension fund. 'Four thousand, three hundred and eighty-two pounds, fifty-five pence, came in today!' Everyone gasped and hallelujahed. It was exciting to see God daily providing our needs. 'We reached the twenty thousand mark today.'

While it was humbling to be on the receiving end of such generosity, it made me feel wretched to find that the expression of constant gratitude was a chore for which I had insufficient time.

A month passed. The deluge of money moderated. Gratitude became overshadowed by the need for more. All that God had so graciously sent our way was not enough to enable us to meet our obligation to pay for the farm. The joy of receiving loving gifts was lost in the anguish that they were not enough. To make matters worse, we were getting close to the wire. Only four weeks remained till we had to come up with sixty-five thousand pounds. The total received had crept up to twenty-five thousand, and while we all recognised that as a magnificent sum, worthy of thanks, where were we going to find the remaining forty thousand?

'There is nothing else for it,' I announced one morning, during staff coffee break. 'We will just have to borrow the money to complete the purchase and then put Oakley back on the market immediately to pay off the debt.'

Everyone shuffled off to work dispiritedly.

Felicity came to see me in my office. She had that look in her eye, and I knew I was in bad trouble.

'Justyn, you really must be more sensitive to the feelings of the staff. They have worked very hard and prayed their knees off for the money for Oakley, and now you tell them it was all for nothing. What we need to hear from you is encouragement to go on trusting God for great things. "He who has taught us to trust in his name, would not so far have brought us to put us to shame",' she quoted.

Of course, she was quite right. It was not fair of me to lay on the staff, who were in no position to do anything about it, the burdens which were my responsibility to carry. But it was difficult to share with them the encouragements if I had to keep from them the disappointments.

'I believe we will see a big miracle. God will provide. You wait and see.' Thus she admonished and encouraged me.

I wonder how I would feel if they ever invited me to captain a soccer team in the World Cup. I should find it terribly intimidating to have all those superstars looking to me for a lead. I am never likely to find out, but being captain of the Hildenborough team was, I imagine, not too dissimilar. There were all the superstars of faith; David the gardener was in goal; Wendy the receptionist was on the wing; Jill the cook was in mid-field, and Felicity was centre forward. Increasingly, I resented having the ball kicked to me. I felt vulnerable and exposed. I found myself resenting

Felicity and the others. Would they not face up to reality? Could they not see reason? Wasn't it as clear as day that the money was not going to be forthcoming, so why would they not allow me to make a sensible business decision?

We discussed yet another appeal letter to our supporters. Suffering as we did from the British reticence to talk directly about money, someone suggested that we merely request prayer 'that the funds would be forthcoming'.

'That is hypocrisy,' I argued. 'If we want people to pray, then let's ask them to pray. But if we want their money, let's ask for it straight!'

'Oh, but it is their prayers that we rely on, not their giving.'

'Baloney! It's not their prayers that we rely on, or their gifts. It is God we should rely on.'

'But God only acts in response to the prayers of his people.'

'Well, that's not true. Who asked for the sun to rise this morning? I certainly didn't, yet it came up right on schedule.'

'Yes, but when it comes to the variable things of life, he waits till we ask before he gives us what we need.'

'If God only moves in response to our requests, then the final responsibility for success or failure rests with people. I don't feel qualified to carry that heavy a burden. And what's more, if our prayers should be answered then we are the ones who will deserve the credit for having been successful in persuading God to act. "Thank you for your prayers, without which none of this would have been possible." That is how our next appeal letter will sound. So men get the credit while God does all the work!'

'So are you saying we shouldn't pray for things?'

'No. But I am saying that we should be honest with our supporters and not try to exert spiritual blackmail on them by making them pray themselves into feeling guilty enough to send us a gift!'

I went away to conduct a week's youth mission in York, in conjunction with the youth of St Michael-Le-Belfry, where David Watson was still the vicar. I was somewhat daunted at the thought of evangelising in the church of Britain's leading evangelist. As I neared the ancient city, that old 'World Cup' feeling came over me again. Here was a whole church full of champions of faith who would be looking to me for a lead. I took some comfort in the thought that they would not be expecting me to lead them in trusting God for money or new staff members. All they wanted of me was to preach the gospel, and I felt that I could manage that, for each week at Hildenborough I was preaching and still seeing numbers responding. Maybe I might be able to teach them a thing or two. After all, David Watson didn't have a monopoly on evangelism.

I was welcomed into one of their 'communities', a home in which several single people lived as though one family. They were very kind to me and did their best to make me feel at home. However, they failed. It was none of their fault, for their goodness to me was genuine and warm. Their trust in God was impressive, but threatening. It seemed that they trusted him for just about everything. Some of the things which they were trusting for struck me as things which they might be better advised to work for. Heat was obviously one of those things for which they were still trusting, for it was conspicuous by its absence. Maybe their trust kept them warm, but it did nothing for

me. Or maybe I was just a thin-blooded southerner, unused
to northern winters. It snowed or sleeted all week, and the
only place I could find any kind of relief was in bed. I was
miserable.

The meetings were pretty frosty as well. I felt like an
intruder. A truckload of coal delivered to Newcastle might
have felt more needed, for when your vicar is an inter-
nationally recognised evangelist, who needs a southern
no-name import? I felt threatened, so preached badly. I
needed to impress, so didn't.

The only thing of significance to happen that week had
nothing to do with the mission. Joy phoned.

'Jay! We have received a phone call from a lady called
Margaret Stewart. She is very keen to talk to you and wants
you to call her as soon as you can.' She relayed to me the
number.

'Any news of Max?'

'Yes, Sue called last night to say that Max is out of
traction and they have had him up and sitting in a chair.'
This was progress indeed.

'How about the financial situation? Any large gifts come
in since I left?'

There was no progress to report in this department, no
prospect of relief from the dilemma we were in. We still
needed forty thousand pounds, and the deadline was just
short of three weeks away.

I put through a long-distance call to Margaret Stewart,
whose name was vaguely familiar to me for some reason.

'Can you remember who I am?' asked the Scottish accent
at the other end of the line. Then it clicked, just in time for
me to be able to reply truthfully, 'Yes, of course!'

Margaret had been with us in Italy at the conference

with Alan Redpath. She had recently been widowed and seemed to have derived much encouragement from the teaching and fellowship that week. Her husband had been something important in the City and by all accounts had left her in no financial shortage.

'How is the extension appeal coming along?' Now that was the kind of question I needed to hear from someone who might be in a position to help!

'OK,' I lied. I had got into trouble from Felicity for pessimism, so I decided to be noncommittal.

'Could you use forty thousand pounds?' Could I use forty thousand pounds! I needed that question even more than the first one. I assured her that we could make good use of such a sum and that, by amazing coincidence, that was the exact sum needed to purchase Oakley Farm.

She explained that she had some money available and that it was laid on her heart to put it in our direction.

'Just how soon do you need it?'

'The completion date on Oakley is in twenty days.' She never faltered. That would pose her no problems at all.

I went to bed and even forgot to shiver. The burden was lifted.

The next day presented an easy schedule, so I took the afternoon off and went for a drive over the Yorkshire Moors. The snow was deep but the roads were clear. The sun shone and everything sparkled with joy. I crammed the car into a snow bank to get it off the road and spent an hour or two wandering along the lanes. The birds sang, the sheep bleated as they foraged in the snow for food. I fully expected to run into James Herriot at any moment. It was good to be alive, after all.

As I walked past the end of a driveway blocked with

snow, I noticed the farm name, half buried: 'Broughton M'. I scraped the snow away. 'Meadows', the obliterated word read.

What about Broughton Manor, I pondered. Maybe there would yet be a happy ending to that saga. If God could turn up trumps at the last moment for the Hildenborough extension, then maybe one day he would make things work out in other ways, too.

'Thank you, Lord, for your faithfulness and your provision. Please forgive my unbelief. Thank you for the faith of all those young people at Hildenborough. Thank you for Felicity and her stubborn determination to trust you.'

I preached better the last few nights of the mission, yet to my knowledge no one became a Christian. I was conscious of the disappointment of the organisers, so it was with some relief that I came to the end of my commitment and headed back south.

On the way home I called in to see Max. He was seated in a wheelchair when I walked in. His white and drawn face behind his straggly ginger beard sparked into a grin. 'Hello, Jay.'

I told him all the news about Margaret Stewart's generous offer. He laughed about my discomfort in York. 'Why do we do this sort of thing?' he mimicked.

Then he told me his news. The feeling was returning in his right side, but he couldn't move his right arm or leg. His left side had no feeling but increasing mobility.

'When will you be walking?' I queried.

'Jay, the likelihood of that is slim. To my knowledge only three people have ever walked out of this ward in the last twenty-five years.'

'So how long will they keep you shut up in here?'

'If I work hard on my physio I should be home by the end of January.'

There was light at the end of the tunnel, albeit grey.

'Jay, I have got a great idea. How about PACE doing a concert right here in Stoke? There is absolutely nothing for the patients to do, except watch telly, so there'd be a huge turn-out. You could give one of your talks, but perhaps shorter than usual!'

Next day, back at the Hildenborough staff coffee break, everyone wanted to know how the mission had gone. 'OK,' I lied, conscious of Felicity's presence. 'But I must tell you about a very significant telephone conversation I had while I was away.'

'Didn't I tell you to trust God to do great things?' Good old Felicity.

Then I shared Max's vision for a PACE concert at Stoke Mandeville Hospital. Agreement was immediate and enthusiasm was high.

But later that day came another phone call from Margaret Stewart. On advice from her accountant, she would be loaning us the money, rather than making it an outright gift. But she assured me that there would be no question of the sum being recalled at an embarrassing moment, so we could count on it for as long as we should need it.

I have an aversion to borrowing money. So this news was something of a disappointment. But all was not lost. We could still go ahead and complete the purchase in two weeks' time. Gift or loan, it was the exact sum needed at precisely the right time. Could it be anything other than the Lord's provision? Nevertheless, I kept the change from the staff for fear of disappointing them and incurring the wrath of Felicity.

One week later, we arrived at the hospital with mounds of amplifying equipment. Several members of the Hildenborough staff had come along to cheer on the members of PACE. It took a good hour to manhandle the heavy equipment into the physiotherapy department, where the concert was billed to take place. Phil muffled his drums with towels so as to avoid disturbing the whole hospital. Dave miraculously refrained from destroying the racks of medical equipment that lined the walls.

The strains of Bob's synthesiser filtering through the hallways seemed to call forth the audience like the Pied Piper of Hamelin. The passages approaching the physiotherapy department were soon jammed with wheelchairs, beds on wheels and people on crutches. Max was in the front row. He looked a little nervous, but quickly relaxed to the familiar songs that he had performed himself on so many occasions. I watched his hands and his useless fingers resting limply in his lap. He'd never play a guitar again.

Then it was my turn to give my 'short talk'. I had practised it many times so I would not waffle. 'Before I start, I want to call upon a very famous recording artist to sing one song for us. He may be a little rusty as he hasn't sung for some time, but he's here tonight and I'd like you to give a big hand for Max Sinclair.' Everyone knew Max, so the applause was spontaneous.

I pushed a startled Max out to the front in his wheelchair and borrowed Dave's guitar. Together we sang our party piece, 'The Cat Came Back'. With Max singing from his wheelchair, the humorous song about a cat that kept bouncing back from one disaster after another took on a whole new significance!

Then I spoke to the assembly on suffering. 'Though God has not intervened to remove it from the world, yet he has entered the world and has suffered as much as any of us through crucifixion. Jesus knows what it is to suffer,' I assured them. 'He understands what it is like to have arms and legs nailed down in helpless redundancy.'

Max had many searching conversations during the following days.

Another phone call came from the lady with the Scottish accent. It seemed that her accountant was jealous to guard her interests, and he hoped that in view of the large sum she would be loaning to the Hildenborough Trust, the Trustees might favourably consider the possibility of offering her a place on the Board.

Something in me rebelled, but not in time to spoil the sweetness of my agreement to put the idea to the chairman at the next meeting, which wasn't till June. It just didn't seem at all right that someone could virtually buy their way on to the Board of Trustees. Surely it was all a matter of trust. The Christian life was all about trust, trusting God and trusting each other.

Yet with one week to go before the deadline, there was no way I was going to rock the boat. The next Trustees' meeting was months away, and anyway the likelihood of their agreeing to such a proposal was slim. I would leave the matter on ice till then.

The staff were excited about their new home, only a week away, but the edge of my excitement was lost. Something was not quite right. My unease grew to concern, which broke out into a rash of worry as the week progressed and no money arrived from Margaret Stewart.

In fact, the money never did come. Maybe she had a change of heart, or maybe her cautious accountant got the better of her. Either way, I was left holding a forty-thousand-pound baby.

So with a few hours to go till completion I went to see the bank manager, cap in hand.

'Stupid Christians,' I imagined him saying. 'They are irresponsible because they confuse business with faith.'

Trust in God's provision did not form part of the contract with the bank, who wanted something more tangible than that, and more expensive.

6

Seeing is Believing

Good news of Max. The Duchess of Kent had graced his ward with her royal presence. Ever the gentleman, and to everyone's amazement, Max had hoisted himself to his feet to shake her hand.

'Mr Sinclair is making unusual progress,' the doctor had told her. 'He'll be walking again in a month or so.' The news was so overwhelming and unexpected that Max had nearly collapsed at the Duchess's feet!

Hot on the heels of the report of Max's 'unusual progress' came news of amazing miracles in Tunbridge Wells.

'Justyn, you really must go. Last night we saw a lady healed of cancer, and another man with a bad heart was healed. It was wonderful, just like being back in the early days of the Church. The atmosphere was so full of a sense of the presence of the Lord that you felt you could just reach out and touch him. Oh, and Sally and Paul got slain in the spirit.'

'Slain in the spirit! What on earth does that mean?'

'Well, they went to the front, and the preacher laid hands on them and they fell down on the ground.'

This was long before Toronto Airport had been placed on the spiritual map, so it sounded like a wrestling match to me. But curiosity beckoned and I went.

The church was jammed. The singing was joyful and enthusiastic and very long, everyone standing to sing one song after another for the better part of an hour. I was impressed with the genuineness of the devotion of the worshippers. They seemed oblivious of those around them, raising their hands to the Lord in love and supplication, sometimes weeping, sometimes laughing out loud. I envied their freedom from self-consciousness in their overriding awareness of the Lord himself. As an Anglican with Brethren roots, I had difficulty even lifting my hands above my shoulders.

'Be like a tree,' urged the song leader, 'and lift your arms to the Lord. Don't sit there like a stump of dead wood.'

I sat there like a stump of dead wood. It wasn't so much rebellion as a natural aversion to calling attention to myself. Children's choruses with actions had always turned me off as a child. I hated 'Wide, wide as the ocean', not for its theology, but for the gesticulations which inevitably accompanied it. I gradually became aware that the shoe was on the wrong foot. I was as conspicuous as a sore thumb, or rather, as a stump in a forest of branch-waving trees. I half-raised one arm.

The preacher reminded us that Jesus had come to do the will of the Father and that the will of the Father had been to heal the sick and raise the dead and cast out demons. If we wanted to be doing the Father's will we had better get doing similar things. 'Greater works than these shall you do also,' Jesus had promised his disciples.

Next, all who had ailments of any kind were called out to the front. I was fascinated to see the aisles jammed with eager people. This was great. Of course God answered prayer, and what could be more natural than for crowds to respond to such an invitation?

The couple in the row in front of me had been nursing an obviously unwell child throughout the somewhat lengthy preliminaries. This was clearly the moment for which they had been waiting. They moved out into the aisle to stand in the ever lengthening line up to the front.

There was nothing secret about what was going on. As people seeking healing reached the preacher at the front of the line, the conversation was amplified through the speaker system to the whole assembly. 'And what do you want God to do for you today?' A man at the front of the line made no reply. Then a friend pushed forward and told the preacher that the man was deaf and wanted to be healed. Ah! That explained his lack of response. The preacher prayed loud enough for the deaf man to hear, so I was sure the Lord would have no difficulty. Then he asked, 'Now can you hear?' No response. So he raised his voice a little and tried again. Still nothing.

'Brother, why don't you go over there and sit down with a member of my team who will pray for you some more.' The man didn't hear but responded to being led by the arm to a vacant pew at the side of the church. There the team member continued with the man for some time in earnest prayer. All the while, others were receiving ministry.

Eventually the couple with the child reached the front of the line. The mother was clearly emotionally keyed up, for she released what was on her heart with a gush. Much prayer with shaking and moaning followed. People all over the auditorium started to weep. Someone released a piercing scream. I felt my spine crawling. 'Be at peace,' soothed the preacher. 'The enemy doesn't like this kind of thing, but God is in control. "If your son asked you for a fish would you give him a serpent? Then if you who are evil know how to give good gifts to your children, how much more will your Heavenly Father give the Holy Spirit to those who ask him?" '

That certainly seemed reasonable and biblical. So I waited to see what would happen. Nothing that I could detect did happen.

'He is healed!' pronounced the preacher. 'Do you believe that your child is whole?' he asked the parents.

'Yes, we do.'

What else could they say? If they said 'no', then they would look foolish and might risk the efficacy of what was taking place. 'Be it unto you according to your faith' made it vital to believe. The child's health depended upon it.

But when they sat down the child didn't look any better.

I returned to gazing around at what was going on. The deaf man had disappeared, presumably having resumed his seat. I wondered if he had been healed.

People were still going up to the front for spiritual ministry. People were being slain in the spirit and were falling to the floor like skittles in a bowling alley.

'No one was ever saved by scepticism,' said the preacher. 'It is faith that saves and faith that heals.'

A woman's voice cried out from the back: 'Thus saith the Lord. I the Lord will heal my people, all those who put their trust in me. So be not faithless but believing.'

The last thing I wanted was to doubt the promises of the Lord. Yet I found myself trapped in a terrible dilemma. I was being presented with the word of the Lord, the believing of which promised healing, the doubting of which would be an insult to God. Yet the things which were taking place before my eyes were as invisible as the Emperor's new clothes. There was nothing to see. I believed God could heal, because it was written in the Bible. Hearing was believing. But if, on the other hand, seeing was believing and my faith was to depend on the evidence of my eyes, then my faith was in trouble. At a magic show 'the quickness of the hand deceives the eye', but here the eye was not being fooled one bit. There was nothing to see. If the eye was not being fooled, then perhaps the heart was.

It occurred to me that perhaps this explained why Jesus was always down on people who sought a sign in order that they might believe. Presumably he was wise to man's predisposition to look at the extraordinary with a view to explaining it rather than with a view to believing it. After all, the world has always argued that seeing is believing, while the Bible has consistently said that faith comes by hearing the word of God. Perhaps our hearts, where faith resides, are more attuned to our ears than to our eyes. The promises which we hear find welcome in faith's abode, but the signs which we see are diverted into the analytical section of our consciousness.

Whatever the explanation, I found myself feeling like an unbeliever in an evangelistic meeting. I seriously wanted to believe what was being promised, for instant healing was a very attractive proposition. But I found it hard to reject the evidence of my eyes and the consequent scepticism of my mind.

Another thing that troubled me was that there were several people I knew up at the front, flat on the floor, slain in the spirit. Either they had much more faith than I, or they were more gullible. To say that they were gullible would be to insult them and to breach fellowship. I had always understood the Bible to teach that we should humbly consider others better than ourselves. Branding my friends 'gullible' would hardly be consistent with that teaching. Yet if I recognised them as having more faith than I, then why would I not join them?

Parked in the aisle next to me was a wheelchair supporting a hunched-over, withered lady.

'I've been here every night this week,' she told me in a loud whisper.

'How long have you been unable to walk?' I asked.

'Twenty-one years.'

'How are you enjoying the services?'

'Very inspirational.'

'But how does it make you feel to see people all around you being healed, yet here you still are in a wheelchair?'

She hesitated for a long time. 'To tell you the truth, it makes me miserable. I have learned to live with my disability; in fact, through it I have drawn very close to God. But now suddenly I am beginning to think that it must be my lack of faith which has kept me here all these years. My enjoyment of his company has perhaps been a selfish thing.'

I felt very sad for her. Surely the demand to have faith should not be conveyed in such a way as to replace an attitude of contentment with one of guilt.

I was still turning the question over in my mind as I slipped out for a breather during one of the hymns. In an alleyway behind the church building I encountered a young man in an obvious state of agitation, or maybe the Spirit of God was strongly upon him.

'You are the Lord's servant, aren't you?' he hailed me as I attempted to walk past. I was flattered at the thought that he might be right, so I stopped.

'Ask whatever you want and he will give it to you,' he said, shaking like a leaf in an earthquake.

I pondered and then replied: 'I want him. To love God and his Son, the Lord Jesus Christ, is all that I desire.'

'But don't you want him to bestow on you a gift of healing or prophecy?'

'I am happy for him to do so, but I am content in him, for he is all I desire.' He looked disappointed.

I returned to the service and heard the preacher tell us that if you want any of the spiritual gifts you have to 'grovel like an animal' for them. 'Earnestly desire the best gifts,' he urged. 'Don't just sit passively by lest the Gift-giver pass you by.'

My smug answer to the man outside instantly convicted me. Should I run back and tell him I'd changed my mind? I didn't know what to do, so I sat tight. When in doubt, do nowt!

By now there was a fresh line of seekers patiently waiting their turn with the preacher at the front of the church. I noticed the deaf man was once again in the line. Maybe this would be decisive. If this man were healed, then maybe it would help me to find the faith which was lacking in me.

When he reached the front of the line the preacher immediately recognised him. 'This is the brother who was healed of his deafness,' he announced to the assembly. 'Now what do you want God to do for you this time?' he enquired of the man.

'I beg your pardon,' stammered the man. 'Only I don't hear so good. You see, I'm deaf.'

Max was released from hospital at the end of January. The first day he made an appearance at Hildenborough Hall was dramatic. No one knew he was home. The dining hall was full of people, many of whom knew and loved Max. They had been praying for his healing for six solid months. Conversation gradually faded away and a great hush fell over the room as he entered, leaning on Sue's arm. Then pandemonium! People cheered and clapped and hallelujahed and rose to their feet in standing ovation. Tears flowed freely; in fact, I doubt there was a dry eye as he painstakingly dragged himself the full length of the room. But he was walking! ('My own individualistic style,' as he called it.) That must surely be a miracle. Max had become the fourth person with his kind of injury to walk out of the spinal unit of Stoke Mandeville Hospital in twenty-five years.

7

Has God Lost His Touch?

'The secret room is still here,' called an excited voice from somewhere upstairs.

'There are no rabbits in the garden,' came another, tinged with disappointment. 'Perhaps they only come out in the summer. Do rabbits hibernate?'

We were back in the Northumberland farmhouse for the Easter holidays. To make it better yet, the Sinclairs were coming to join us for a few days.

Once home, the weeks of readjustment to normal living back in the real world had proved painful for Max, perhaps more so than the six months in hospital. There he had been making steady progress, progress which was greater than that of almost any of the other patients. But at home he was a cripple, unable to cope with even some of the simplest of daily tasks.

Now it was good to think of a whole week together. We arrived a few days before them to get things prepared. Excitement knew no bounds as their Ford Granada nosed its way up the drive.

The children disappeared immediately to disclose the secret of the hidden room to Naomi and Anna.

How strange it was to sit there with Max and Sue, sipping coffee beside the very telephone which had shattered our peace so completely nine months previously. Max had not died. He was here, his old humorous self. Or was he himself?

We talked through all the things we had not had time to discuss for months. We were fascinated to learn that the very day of the accident, the day we had been so much at peace here in Norham, Max and Sue had been praying that God would help them decide how to make the rest of their lives truly count in his service. Doubtless they would never have chosen the changes which resulted, but it amazed me to see just how peaceful they both were in full acceptance that what had taken place was a definite answer to their prayer. They didn't see it as an accident at all.

'Do you mean to tell me that you think that God did that to you?'

'No. But he must have allowed it, for nothing happens without his permission. Quite what his reasons were we don't yet know. Maybe we'll never know. But we are happy to trust that he knows best.'

I told them about my experience in Tunbridge Wells. 'Wouldn't you like to be completely healed, Max? That preacher told us that all illness is out of line with the will of God because it is imperfect. Jesus healed people when he was on earth to restore them to perfection.'

'Strange to say, we have prayed very little about being healed. We have been content to leave that request to others, in confidence that the Lord will answer as he thinks best.'

I told them about the lady in the wheelchair. 'She was coming to the conclusion that it was her lack of faith that had kept her disabled for so long.'

Sue interjected: 'Just the other day we heard of a group of Christians who were meeting in Exeter on the day of the accident. When they heard what had happened to us they sat up all night praying for Max's healing. But about three o'clock in the morning they apparently sensed a blockage. They said it was as if God was saying, "I can do no more because of Max's unbelief." So they stopped praying at that point.'

'I find that hard to swallow,' I said. 'If God is like that then he is cruel!'

It rained a lot, as it often does in Northumberland, so we played endless snooker, a game at which I had never been able to beat Max till then. It was only his determination which kept him at it in the face of repeated defeat! But after a couple of days the rain stopped and we grabbed the opportunity to take a trip.

Bamburgh Castle stood rock-like amid the sand dunes of the Northumberland coast. The sea had withdrawn its presence by half a mile down a glistening expanse of sand. The children erupted from the car and raced towards the water's edge. Joy and I followed more slowly. Halfway down the beach we turned to see what progress Max and Sue were making. They were still struggling through the sand dunes below the castle wall. There was the walking miracle, hailed by many as a shining example of God's healing power.

It must have been the vast expanse of sand which emphasised Max's disability by presenting him with so great an impossibility. In every other situation he had been encouraged by his increasing mobility. He could handle first a wheelchair and then a stick. He could write, answer the telephone, hold a conversation, speak in a meeting, drive a car, even lose at snooker. But he could not run down a beach with his children. Was this really a miracle?

We walked sadly back to meet them and contented ourselves with sitting in the dunes, sheltered from the blast of the wind from the North Sea.

When the children came panting back, we set out to explore the castle. Max would be able to manage that more easily than dragging his leg through the sand. We set the children loose on the old hunt-the-treasure routine. It was amazing how careless those ancient Brits had been, and extraordinary that those fivepenny pieces should have lain so long undiscovered, particularly when you consider that the Scottish border was only a few miles distant!

The older children began to smell a rat when they examined the dates on the coins. 'Daddy put it there.' 'No! It was Uncle Max.'

Santa might have been another possible candidate. Perhaps that was why prayers so often seemed to go unanswered. Daddy wasn't around to provide. Maybe GOD was but an acrostic for Good Old Dad. That would explain Max's far from adequate recovery, the non-appearance of the needed funds to pay for the farmhouse, Broughton Manor and my own failure as a preacher and conference director.

I don't know when this hypothesis surfaced in my conscious thoughts, yet as I began to turn it over in my mind, I realised it was no stranger. It had lurked at the back of my mind for months. It had probably been in the 'pending file' of my thoughts, labelled 'work on this when there is time to think'. When every day for months on end presents impossible deadlines, files like that get neglected. There had been no time for the luxury of considering such issues as 'Does God answer prayer?' or 'Does he even hear prayer in the first place?' or 'Is God there at all?' But that is the trouble with holidays. They give you time to think, and thinking can be dangerous.

The Sinclairs went home the following day. I think it was all a bit too much for Max. But the quietness they left behind them left me with more time than ever to think.

I went out to pray over this possible explanation for my increasing sense of disquiet. I always talked everything over with the Lord, and found no greater joy than a walk over open ground with only the Creator for company. But this time it was different. How could I talk to God about the possibility of his non-existence? For an unbeliever to raise the tentative question of his reality was a positive step in the right direction. This was the opposite. If he was really listening, then such a suggestion would have been insulting in the extreme, and you can't enjoy a walk with a friend while you insult him. And if he was not there, then talking to him was little more than madness, or self-deception. I tried to pray but it was useless, so I returned to the farmhouse.

'What's wrong, Jay?' Joy could read me like a book. 'You don't seem yourself.'

Should I tell her what I was thinking? At least I could be sure that Joy was real and my talking it over with her could not be mistaken for madness. 'Let's take a walk.'

We headed off down the lane in the drizzling rain.

'You have been terribly quiet these past days. Even the Sinclairs must have noticed that you were not your usual cheerful self. What is going on in your head?'

'Joy, I hardly know what to say.' Joy looked very white

and it occurred to me that she must have been wondering if I was having an affair. So I hurried on. 'You will probably think I am mad, but I cannot escape from the recurring thought that, just maybe, we are fooling ourselves in our belief in God.'

Lightning didn't flash, nor thunder roll. The stone walls beside the road didn't crumble. The sheep didn't even look up from their grazing. Joy said nothing.

'It has been so long since we have seen anything even remotely resembling an answer to prayer. Max's recovery is the next best thing, but seeing him struggling through the sand dunes by Bamburgh Castle made me wonder about the rightness of attributing the credit to God.'

Joy could have rationalised that God always answers prayer, but sometimes the answer is 'no'. Mercifully she didn't irritate me with clichés. She just listened and understood.

To have voiced my question gave birth to it, made it official, brought it out into the open, gave it diplomatic status. It was no longer an outlawed intruder. I now owned it, even gave it a degree of credibility. Immediately, it grew.

Eventually, we too had to get back to work. There I did my best to return the newborn monster to its cage, but it was no use. It was loose and it was growing.

I tried to bury it under all the pressing matters which needed attention. The newly acquired staff house, Oakley Farm, had to be modernised for occupation by the staff, and some of the land and buildings had to be divided off for resale in order to pay off the indebtedness to the bank. The staff shortage was as acute as ever, but Felicity Lane was doing a great job holding things together. The summer season was approaching and that required much planning. Each weekend was full of young people eager to get to know God or to grow in their Christian experience. More often than not, I was the main speaker. There was no way I could let on, even for a moment, that I questioned the truth I was preaching. But the questions refused to be buried. The pending file was on my mental desk-top and refused to be shoved to one side.

How could I find the time to do some serious thinking? Why not teach one weekend on the subject of doubt? That way, I would have to think things through in an orderly manner so that I could present them to others. All being well, I would come up with a solution to the questions and that would be the end of the matter. After all, if God cared at all about his own reputation he would have to help me find some answers to present, or he might find the debate going the wrong way.

The result was disappointing. My presentation was unconvincing. The teaching sessions dragged to a boring conclusion, or perhaps a 'boring end' might be a better description, for the nearest anyone came to a conclusion was my own growing conviction that the doubts had more validity than the evidence for faith.

When everyone had gone home and Hildenborough returned to its silent, empty self, I set off for a walk in the rain. Once out of earshot of everyone but the rabbits, I tried to pray. It was useless. An expression of doubt makes a prayer of faith a contradiction. Then I got mad. I couldn't talk with God in simple friendship, so I shouted at him in rage. Yes, I feared his displeasure, but if God were real and loved me as the Bible taught me, then he would understand.

Maybe if I were abusive enough, I could bait him into punishing me. Then his reaction would convince me of his reality. The punishment might be easier to take than the uncertainty.

But there was no response. Nothing.

I had read of an atheist who, one hundred years ago, challenged God to a duel in London's Hyde Park. There the man had stood, with drawn sword, but when God didn't show, he sheathed his weapon in the conclusion that his atheism was justified. Just then an insect flew into his eye, causing an irritation which grew till the man died.

But there were no flies out that day.

'*Distress and anguish fill him with terror; they overwhelm him, because he shakes his fist at God and vaunts himself against the Almighty, defiantly charging against him with a thick, strong shield.*' Job knew how I felt.

'O God,' I cried in anguish. 'I know that you are terribly great and in comparison I am nothing. I know that even if you do exist, there is so much to occupy you that I see no reason why you should even be aware of my existence, let alone take time to listen to my prayer. The reason I pray has nothing to do with my presumption. I pray simply because you told us to do so. It is illogical that you should want us to pray and unreasonable for us to presume on your attention. Nevertheless, you have said that you will grant anything we ask in your name. Well, what went wrong over Broughton Manor? Why did you so let down those young people on the staff who prayed for the money to pay for Oakley Farm? It was I who was left looking stupid just because you failed to keep your promise. And what about Max? If that is the best you can do by way of a healing in

the twentieth century, then you must be losing your touch.'
I went on and on, sometimes weeping, sometimes shouting
in rage.

But there was no response.

8

Confession is Good for the Soul

Knole Park in Sevenoaks is magnificent. Huge old beech trees stand out of the bracken. Deer flit through the glades or graze in herds on open meadows. Knole House itself stands witness to centuries of change, carrying into the present a sense of timelessness.

Joy and I made it something of a weekly tradition on a Monday morning to walk through the park to the Buck's Head in Godden Green, where we would replenish our depleted energy with a ploughman's lunch.

'What do you think I should do?' I asked Joy as we walked. I hadn't confided my doubt to anyone but her. 'These questions just don't seem to be going away.'

'I think you should talk it over with someone you trust.'

'That's just what I am doing.'

'No. You should talk to someone else.'

'Well, who do you suggest?' The theory was good, but in reality all the people I might naturally have turned to in those circumstances were in Heaven, and so unavailable for a confidential chat. No wonder King Saul yielded to the temptation of calling up from the dead the departed spirit of Samuel. But in view of the fact that the very next day Saul had died, I decided to seek my counsel from the living!

'How about Alan Redpath?' Joy suggested.

Now that was an inspiration. He was friend enough to confide in, wise enough to advise me aright, and lived far enough away not to start a rumour.

'Yes. Uncle Alan is just the right person.'

Next morning my Bible reading led me to Psalm 73. It was encouraging to find that even psalm writers suffered from second thoughts from time to time. '*How can God know? Does the Most High have knowledge? Surely in vain have I kept my heart pure; in vain have I washed my hands in innocence.*' Yet this psalm indicated that the writer had checked himself before expressing his misgivings out loud. '*If I had said, "I will speak thus," I would have betrayed your children.*'

Yes, that was the trouble. If I were to voice my own doubts, then I would be guilty of betraying my fellow Christians. There must have been dozens of young people who had found faith through my preaching. What would happen to them if ever they heard that Justyn Rees no longer believed what he had preached to them?

A cross-reference in the margin of my Bible took me to Job, where the wretched man's friends had told him to watch his mouth. '*Think how you have instructed many. Your words have supported those who stumbled; But now trouble comes to you, and you are discouraged; Should not your piety be your confidence?*' I supposed that if I were to speak openly of my doubts, I could expect similar advice from my friends.

So I followed up another cross-reference, which led me to the epistle of James: '*Not many of you should presume to be teachers, my brothers, because you know that we who teach will be judged more strictly.*' It was too late to avoid the presumption of teaching others. The damage was already done. '*The tongue is a small part of the body, but it makes great boasts.*' That's right. Thoughts are my own affair, but once the tongue starts wagging it affects others. '*Take ships as an example. Although they are so large and are driven by strong winds, they are steered by a very small rudder wherever the pilot wants to go. Consider what a great forest is set on fire by a small spark.*' So my words would not only have the destructive potential of a forest fire, but would also set a direction for my own life as the rudder sets the course for the whole ship. If I verbalised doubt, then that would be the direction in which my life would go. And, like a fire ship, I would leave behind me a trail of disaster.

I resolved, therefore, to say nothing. If we could get more help with running Hildenborough then perhaps I could get my head together. What we needed was a new chaplain and a business administrator. While Felicity was doing a great job holding the office together, I needed someone who could give overall leadership to the physical and business operation of the centre. Hildenborough could ill afford the extra salaries but it could afford even less an agnostic director. So I placed the advertisements. Some big changes had to be made.

Days went by. Six weekend conferences came and went. I taught the truth as the Bible tells it, not as I believed it. I declined to preach the gospel on the Saturday open evenings. Teaching the truth was one thing, but calling people to have faith in Jesus was quite another. I handed over this responsibility to the PACE team.

One Saturday evening they presented a concert in the open air. Hundreds came, and the great courtyard in front of the main entrance door of Hildenborough Hall was a mass of excited young people. Joy was busy catering in the kitchen. PACE were busy preparing for the concert. Felicity was in the office. I was there as front man to welcome everyone and to get things generally organised. Everyone was so friendly.

'How are you?'

'Fine, thanks, and you?'

'Isn't it great to see all these young people here this evening?'

'Yes, it's lovely . . .' But that was not what I was thinking inside. 'NO! I wish they would all go away and leave me alone instead of coming here and demanding faith.'

I couldn't keep the pretence up for long. I introduced PACE with the usual act, then fled to the secrecy of our apartment. I locked the door and turned up the television. But the concert was just outside my window, and PACE took seriously the psalmist's injunction to 'make a joyful *noise* unto the Lord'. The television was no match for the gospel decibels. I thought of going out for a walk, but there was no way to escape unobserved as my front door opened in full view of the courtyard, and the back way passed by the office, where Felicity would witness my departure. In any case, I was responsible for a house full of several hundred teenagers and, God or no God, I couldn't just abandon my post. Shame and duty imprisoned me in our apartment.

I listened as Harold brought the evening to a close with a challenge to trust Christ as personal saviour.

'What a con!' I found myself muttering. 'All these innocent kids being misled into believing something which just isn't true.' Then I found myself angry, not just with

God, because he probably didn't exist anyway, but with Christians who were perpetuating the lie, and, in particular, with the PACE team for so eloquently and convincingly encapsulating the lie I had preached to so many but could never preach again. I hid in the apartment for the rest of the evening, not answering the bell or the phone, lest someone should ask me a question I might be unable to lie back to.

Next day things regained some of their proper perspective. My cynicism had overdone it the previous evening. But I was worried at the intensity of my feelings. Something had to be done. I resolved to go and see Alan Redpath at the earliest convenience.

'Hello, Justyn,' crackled Uncle Alan's voice over the phone. 'How are you doing?'

'Not so good.' The truth at last. 'I need some advice. Could I pop up to see you?'

'By all means, Justyn. When would you like to come?'

'What are you doing tomorrow?'

'Is it that urgent?'

We set up the meeting. I made convincing excuses to Felicity to cover my tracks, for I certainly didn't want anyone guessing at my intentions. I felt like a kid playing hooky from school or an alcoholic hiding a bottle.

I boarded a train to Carnforth and settled down in a window seat with a notebook. I used the journey to set down in an orderly fashion the matter I wanted to lay before the sage. I still have the notebook and so can recall exactly what I wrote:

I doubt the practical experience of God's working in my life and that of others.

I particularly doubt God's willingness to guide us in everyday things and to provide our needs of staff and finance.

I can pray, provided I don't think too hard what I am doing and that I don't pray specifically for practical things.

I am irritated by a spiritual approach to practical problems. This is especially apparent among those who prefer 'living by faith' to hard work.

I am browned off with Christians with problems (like me!). Why can't we get on with living without constant self-analysis?

I then added in small letters, as though, if I wrote it very small or said it very quietly, it might not be so bad:

Is God real?

Then followed some definite, practical questions to which I wanted answers:

Am I running a business or a faith enterprise?
Should I resign?

If I were to resign from Hildenborough, would that be giving in to the temptation not to believe?

If I stay on at Hildenborough, would that be lack of faith? After all, what else would I do for a living?

Should I continue to act, or should I tell all and risk confidence being lost in Hildenborough?

How can I slip out of Christian leadership unobtrusively without upsetting the faith of others?

Is it possible to retain enough Christianity to make sense of living without having to have faith?'

* * *

I felt towards that little notebook as does a choirboy reading a dirty book during the sermon. There were all the secrets of my heart, which I had only recently admitted to myself, all set down on paper. What if anyone should ever read it? I should have died at the thought of it being published in a book.

The train pulled into Carnforth and abandoned me on the platform. I telephoned the Redpaths to let them know that I had arrived, then settled down on a bench in the early summer sun to wait for a ride.

All at once I felt desperately alone. I was a long way from home. This was unfamiliar territory. I was on an errand of unfaithfulness to all I had stood for all my life. I had no right to be there. I felt like a man about to commit adultery against his wife. I was on the point of running when the Redpaths drove up.

We chatted of this and that as we drove the few miles to the grounds of Capernwray Hall, where they lived. The Italy conference had been good. No, he hadn't been doing any more mountaineering. Max was much improved, walking without a stick though he still had no feeling in one side of his body and very limited movement in the other. Yes (without conviction), it did smack of the miraculous. No, I wasn't planning any exciting new ventures for the autumn season. Yes, Mother was very well, thank you.

Then we were driving through the stately grounds of Capernwray. Capernwray was a conference centre, much like Hildenborough. In fact, it had been started at much the same time. My father had founded Hildenborough in 1945 and Ian Thomas opened shop the following year. They had retained informal links ever since. I had been there several times before, but on those occasions I had come in peace. Everything looked much the same, except that for once it was not raining. The clean-cut young people who formed the student body of the Torchbearers Bible School all looked very impressive and earnest.

'Are they all just fooling themselves?' I asked myself. 'Are they just viewing life through the rose-tinted spectacles of the optimism of youth? No wonder they all look so confident. They know all the answers to all the questions life has ever posed to them. Just wait . . .'

Over tea we continued the small talk. Yes, Joy and the children were fine. Hildenborough was indeed flourishing, and people were continuing to become Christians in encouraging numbers. No, the expansion programme was not going ahead.

Then, mercifully, the teapot was dry and we could get down to the meat of the matter. With years of instinctive tact, Marjorie had chores to attend to in the kitchen and withdrew, leaving Alan and me alone on the patio in the sun with the sweet peas and the scent of new-mown grass.

The moment had come to speak. The match was struck. The forest was dry. The ship awaited the tiller's redirection. Alan Redpath was all ears.

'I have lost my faith. I don't know if I believe in God any more.'

I could never take those words back. I had confessed. It was no longer a secret.

Alan Redpath didn't appear to be in the least shaken. In all his years I suppose he must have listened to hundreds of similar confessions. With the disclosure came a sense of relief, and soon the whole story came tumbling out. It must have sounded disjointed and confused, but that was a pretty fair impression of how I was feeling.

'So what am I to do?' I concluded. 'If I admit my doubts then I will damage the faith of many young people involved with Hildenborough. Yet I cannot go on pretending.'

'The best advice I can give you is to be honest and open. The Bible says, "If we walk in the light as he is in the light, we can have fellowship with one another." You will find yourself isolated by your secret. What you really need is loving support. No one can give you that while you continue to pretend that all is well.'

He recounted to me a few horror stories of pastors of churches who had hidden their doubts for years.

'But what about Psalm 73 and James 3?' I quoted the passages which had kept me mute the previous weeks.

'There is a world of difference between asking an honest question and making a definite statement. Part of the responsibility of leadership is honesty. Your secrecy in this matter may soon turn to hypocrisy if you are not very careful.'

'What should I do if the doubts persist? I cannot go on directing a faith venture indefinitely while everyone knows that I don't believe.'

'Set deadlines for the problems to be resolved. When must you have the full complement of staff in place for the summer season? When can you reasonably expect to have a business administrator appointed? By what date should a new chaplain be added to the team?

What appealed to me was the way he was offering practical solutions to practical problems. 'Deadlines', 'Appointments'. This was advice worth heeding.

'Why do you think this is happening to me?'

'Three explanations occur to me.' He's a preacher, I

thought. He's bound to have three points. 'Satan may be attacking you, in which case you must resist him. Second, God may be telling you to stop, or at any rate slow down. Third, you may just be suffering from the after-effects of having overworked.'

'May I suggest a fourth possibility? It may be that common sense is showing through at last. Perhaps there is no God after all.'

A discussion of Christian apologetics would have done no good at that juncture. Anyway, I was well versed in all the standard questions and answers.

The interview was inconclusive. I may have expected that having handed over the problem to him, he would somehow be able to remove it from me. Certainly a cure would have been preferable to the prospect of going home to tell all.

On the southbound train I got out my little notebook once again. I titled a fresh page 'Course of action' with a column headed 'Deadlines'.

The members of the Council of Management were all long-standing friends. Tim Giles, for example, had been best man at our wedding. Max was a member. Nigel Cooke was the chairman; I had known him since I was a child. 'Be honest and open' was ringing in my ears. If I was going to start this new policy of openness, then it might as well start right here.

Several members worked in London, so we made it our practice to start with sandwiches to stave off the after-work, fresh-off-the-commuter-train pangs of hunger.

When bodily appetites were satisfied, we started. Nigel Cooke opened with prayer. Bank balances were discussed, just to depress us. A progress report on the agricultural project was presented by David Calcott.

'Now, Justyn, tell us how the conferences are going,' said Nigel, turning all attention on me. This was the moment of disclosure.

I had carefully rehearsed what I was going to tell them. But suddenly I was terrified of hurting these my friends. I felt as one must feel facing the family after a visit to the doctor's at which he has disclosed to you a fatal illness and your inevitable death.

Before I could say a word, I was overcome by grief and horror and sat weeping for several seconds. I felt such a fool. No one said anything. What could they say? I heard coughs, and feet shuffling. Eventually I got a grip of myself and blew my nose. I cleared my throat and mumbled an apology.

'What is on your mind?' Nigel asked kindly.

'I have lost my faith,' I announced simply. Alan Redpath may have been able to hide his reactions but the stunned expressions round the room revealed the inability of the Council members to do likewise.

'What do you mean?'

'I don't know that I believe in God any more.'

'You can't be serious.' But my display of waterworks underscored my sincerity.

'How long has this been going on?'

'Weeks, months, I don't know exactly.' I felt their sympathy, yet was aware that they just couldn't understand. Even Max looked taken aback.

'What are we going to do?'

'I see two options,' I said, trying to redeem my self-respect by grabbing the initiative. 'I must get right away from Hildenborough till my faith returns. Alternatively, I must resign altogether.'

No one doubted the wisdom of our getting away, and agreement was readily reached on that option. But there were still a multitude of practical difficulties to be overcome. Joy and I covered between us the roles of general director, housekeeper, catering supervisor, conference director, chaplain and general buck-stopper. How could all those people be away through the busy summer months?

I confessed to having placed the advertisement for an administrator to which I had received to date two or three replies. I couldn't have told them at a better time! It was agreed to start interviews right away.

The meeting ended early. I felt uneasy. My good friends hadn't understood me. They felt sorry for me, but I wondered if they didn't also feel betrayed by me.

'*A despairing man should have the devotion of his friends, even though he forsakes the fear of the Almighty. But my brothers are as undependable as intermittent streams. They see something dreadful and are afraid.*' I had been right to anticipate the same reaction as Job had received from his friends.

It was several weeks before we did manage to get away. An administrator was appointed to the job on a three-month trial basis. Also, Max was beginning to get back into the work. A year had elapsed since his accident and he was longing to get going again. So he would be at Hildenborough as much as his limited strength would allow. Phil Taylor, a member of the PACE team, agreed to stay on to act as Max's assistant during the summer. Felicity Lane would continue to hold the office together and the assistant cook was quickly getting to grips with the many catering responsibilities. So we were away, and Hildenborough was covered.

Tim Giles had invited us to join his family and a group of friends from his church on a camping holiday in Cornwall. It sounded idyllic, 'grassy field sloping gently down to the water's edge'. So we hitched up our little camping trailer and joined them.

It would have been idyllic but for the hordes of others who had chosen that same field for the same idyllic reasons. Crowds were too like Hildenborough Hall for comfort. All I wanted was to retreat into a deep dark hole where no other humans lurked.

To further aggravate my discomfort, Tim's friends were all Christians. Christians expected faith of one another. But for some unaccountable reason, these good people didn't seem to be making any demands on me whatsoever. The absence of their expectations was even more alarming. Why did they never talk to me about anything of greater importance than the lovely weather we were having? When would the prayer meetings and Bible studies start? Then it dawned on my confused brain that they all knew about me and were being tactful. Knowing Christians as well as I did, I further deduced that the prayer meetings were indeed taking place, but on the quiet. Almost certainly I was being prayed for. I wanted to run. But they were all being so very kind and welcoming that an untimely departure would have been in bad taste. So I stuck it out for several days, feeling as awkward as a non-Christian at a weekend retreat at Hildenborough Hall!

Sunday brought with it the inevitable chore of attending church. Everyone wanted to go to the church of St Just, a beautiful little church set amid the trees right on the water's edge. We went along.

I have attended an Anglican church most of my life, so the liturgy was familiar. But something struck a discord in my soul that morning. Why did they say the same things in the same old-fashioned English they had used for hundreds of years? Why did the vicar and the choir have to dress in those ridiculous clothes? Why on earth go through that strange ritual of gesticulations and hand motions with the bread and wine? Why not just pass it round and get on with it?

I had a ridiculous flash-back to a children's party game in which participants are required to mimic a mime, with no explanation of what they are actually doing. The amusement derived by the audience from the foolish antics of the ignorant actors must surely have been akin to the rapture of the worshippers that morning in the church of St Just. Doubtless Cranmer and his contemporaries had understood what they were about, but subsequent genera- tions were still going through the motions, each one copying the movements of their predecessors while having no idea what they were supposed to mean.

I waited impatiently for the benediction, but when it came it was a disappointment. It was full of flowery poetry and reeked of a mixture of religion and mysticism. I was the first outside into the blessed sunshine and fresh air.

'Wasn't that a lovely service,' bleated one of the group. I couldn't bear it.

'No,' I replied. 'I think it was a mixture of superstition and religious mumbo-jumbo. The whole thing was archaic and unrelated to reality. Indeed, I for one felt most uncomfortable just being there. If that is a true reflection of what God is like, then God must have been dead a very long time.'

It was ungracious of me, but I was following orders: 'Be open and honest.'

But openness is a two-way street, and before I knew it I was swamped with the honest opinions that had been corked by tact till that moment.

'The trouble with you, Justyn, is that you are too narrow in your outlook.'

'What in the world do you mean?'

'You are too obsessed with Hildenborough Hall. That service was not as you would do it at Hildenborough, so you didn't like it. You are too stuck in the tradition of your father.'

So I was narrow, was I? That's what people were thinking. I resented it, most likely because there was truth in the accusation. I had been raised as a child at Hildenborough, and I had been general director for the past eight years. I had become small-minded, shut up in one little world where I was king of the castle.

But they weren't finished with me yet. My tactless disapproval of the service had got under someone's skin, and righteous indignation was released under the banner of honesty.

'There is something else you ought to realise. You are narrow in your outlook in other ways too. You don't drink, so you look down on everyone who does. You are a conservative evangelical, so you are suspicious of every other brand of faith, from charismatic to traditional Anglican. You ought to branch out a little, have some fun, enjoy life and don't be so intense.'

All that sounds a little bald, and in reality it wasn't quite as blunt as that. It was a longish conversation which lasted over lunch and on into the afternoon. But when you distil it, the highlights you are left with sound something less than compassionate.

Those were good friends who had the grace to share with me what was on their minds. The message must have got through, for I still remember what was said. And I have subsequently made adjustments in line with their thinking. They were right, but at the time I resented it, much as Job must have resented the well-intentioned but misguided encouragement of his friends. '*I have become a laughing stock to my friends. Men at ease have contempt for misfortune as the fate of those whose feet are slipping.*'

So next day we left.

We migrated north to the other end of the country, as far away as possible from Cornwall and Hildenborough Hall. We crossed over the sea to Skye and found what we really wanted, seclusion. 'Idyllic' really was the right description this time. We parked our van in a little grassy meadow ablaze with wild flowers. There were rocks on one side, a stream on the other and the sea herself completed our boundary. Across the bay were purple mountains.

The only sounds were the washing of the waves, the bleating of the sheep and the piping of the seabirds. No telephone shattered the silence, threatening our peace with bad news. No friends gave us advice. No staff member looked to me for leadership. No shortage sought its solution in my faith. The mountains made no demands to be cast into the sea. There were plenty of islands already. The sea went about its business, ignoring and accepting us, but never inviting us to walk on its surface. The children discovered the hidden treasures of the rock pools and the wild flowers, while Joy and I had time to think about nothing but today. Yesterday was best forgotten and tomorrow was unattractive. But today was OK.

Four weeks of holiday didn't cure anything, but at least we summoned the zip to face returning to Hildenborough. Our ability to take no anxious thought for the things of the morrow was squeezed by the need to return for the new school term. Becky was to start school for the first time on September 5th and nothing should stand in the path of education.

'We'll go back and try to pick up where we left off. If we ignore the problems, perhaps they'll go away.'

The best of a camping holiday is getting home. After six weeks in a caravan, everything was magic. Running water, even hot running water, electricity, fridge, TV, flush toilet. The cloud of leaving Skye certainly had a silver lining.

But next day the lining faded and the cloud thickened. It was time to go to work.

'Hello, Justyn. Good to see you back. Have you had a good break?' Then came the one I dreaded. 'How are you?' Everyone wanted to know how I was. For once the question was more than a greeting. They really wanted to know. Has he got his head together? Has he got his faith back? No one asked that explicitly, but the question was always there.

I smiled my way to the privacy of my office. Then in came good old Max, hobbling but looking great. He brought me up to date on all the latest developments. The summer conferences had gone without a hitch, except that the new administrator's wife had been seriously ill ever since we had left and so he had never been able to take full control of the centre. The renovations of Oakley Farm were progressing satisfactorily. But the agricultural project was costing more money than it was likely to save.

'This week we have a lovely group of families staying with us. Many of them are very keen to see you and Joy. Is there any chance of you putting in an appearance this evening?'

'Yes, of course, but what do you want me to do? There is no way I could give a talk or anything like that.'

'Let's conduct it as an interview. I'll ask the questions and all you'll have to do is to answer. That way we can't go wrong and you won't have to plan anything.'

I agreed and we showed up at eight o'clock as directed. It felt very strange to be on the platform again, the place where I had preached so many times. I sat quietly and surveyed the smiling faces. They were such a lovely-looking group of people and were so welcoming to us. I wondered if they knew where I was at. Their openness demanded the same of us, but I was not prepared to be 'open and honest' from the Hildenborough platform. So I couldn't be myself, for that would ruin their holiday. I would have to return their genuineness with pretence. But that was unthinkable, so I looked for the door. I was just about to make a dash for cover when Max started in with his questions. It was too late. I just had to go through with it. I resolved to play it dumb. To say as little as possible would limit the number of lies I would have to tell. I gave one-word answers where possible. Max was at a loss to know what to do. The interview fizzled out. Joy was very embarrassed and Max vowed never to interview me again.

A Council of Management meeting was scheduled for the next evening, doubtless timed to coincide with my return. There were decisions to be made which depended to a large extent on my state of mind. No one asked how I was, so I guessed that Max must have been on the telephone earlier in the day.

The meeting was to decide how best to proceed. The new administrator could not continue because of his wife's health. Someone had to take charge. It went without discussion that I was out of action. Max was anxious not to impede his own recovery by taking too much responsibility, so he declined. What were we to do?

'I propose that we close down the operation, at least till next year. By then we will have been able to find the help we need and we won't be driven into the floor just in order to keep open.'

The proposal was readily agreed and I was appointed to the task of organising 'Operation Mothball'.

My first job was to write to all those who were booked to stay with us to tell them that the programme was cancelled.

Next I had to lay off as many of the staff as possible. It would not be so bad for the younger, single members of staff, but for those with families it would mean real hardship. I had them in one by one. Each painful interview increased my depression. Who do you kick when you are fired? The boss, of course. But who does the boss kick? My anger with the God I no longer believed in grew. If he was really so great, why did he allow all these people who trusted in him to be so hurt? And if there was not a God, then who could I kick? Christians were the obvious choice, for they were responsible for perpetuating the deception which could end in this kind of disappointment.

'And so, you see, we have no alternative but to close the place,' I told Felicity Lane. 'It is not yet clear when, or even if, Hildenborough will reopen. So please accept this as the termination of your employment by the Trust.'

The gracious way she accepted the dismissal was my undoing. She showed little or no thought of her own circumstances, but was so obviously concerned for me. Christians could not possibly be at fault, could not be blamed. So God was the guilty one.

The maintenance manager did not accept the dismissal so easily. He had recently moved his whole family from the south coast to take on the maintenance of the property. I didn't blame him for wanting compensation; I wanted it myself. But it was easier to deal with someone who was angry with you for being fired than with someone who reacted with grace. So I returned him frustration for frustration.

With almost everyone gone, it fell to me to do all manner of jobs. Opening the mail one morning, I read a letter from a would-be guest:

Dear Sir,
I awoke in the middle of last night to hear the Lord speaking to me. He told me to go to Hildenborough for the weekend you have planned in mid-October for single people. Please be good enough to reserve me a single room . . .

I wrote back:

Dear Mr . . .
Thank you for your letter requesting accommodation for the weekend in October for singles.
I regret that we are unable to offer you this

accommodation as the centre is closed for the autumn and the programme is cancelled.

How strange that the Lord should have directed you to that weekend when Hildenborough was to be closed. Perhaps he didn't know, or perhaps he just got his wires crossed.

Yours sincerely . . .

9

In Search of God

Once Hildenborough was shut down there was little to be done – no staff to organise, no guests to entertain or preach to, no bucks to be stopped. We moved back into Munda and Joy settled back into the routine of home and motherhood, while the children went happily back to school. I was redundant. So I took the opportunity to get away on my own. I didn't want a holiday. I had just had six weeks. I wasn't running away, because there was nothing to run from. But I did want to get alone to seek God in deadly earnest, just in case he was there to be found, after all.

It was a strange contradiction. I was very cross with a God I thought I didn't believe in, and yet I wanted him more than anything else in life. But what was the sense in wanting him if he didn't exist? There was no solving the equation. Nevertheless, I was resolved to try.

I hitched up the faithful caravan and headed back to the Isle of Skye, where we had known such peace during the summer. Many lovers of the west coast of Scotland have enjoyed the writings of Gavin Maxwell. Through words he manages to paint a picture in the reader's mind of the wild beauty of the place. Often I had found mental escape from the pressures of Hildenborough to the freedom of the

Highlands through *Ring of Bright Water*. Perhaps it was Maxwell who enticed me once again to drag the van those six hundred twisting miles.

I thought at first to return to the same meadow we had occupied a couple of months previously, but decided that a fresh environment would be more conducive to fresh thought. I found another deserted beach on the north coast of the Sleat Peninsula. No one lived nearby, so isolation was guaranteed. Just across the bay were the ruins of a long-abandoned castle, and beyond were the Cuillin Hills, spiky and purple against the sky. The sea washed my doorstep and my only companions were the sheep, cows and a weather-beaten bull whom I named Ferdinand, with dubious originality.

In those circumstances it would have been very easy to have vegetated. However, I was determined to get to grips with the problem and to solve it. I made it a daily habit to rise early and to go for a run, to blow the cobwebs away and in an attempt to get physically more fit. Next, I would have a light breakfast followed by an hour's Bible reading. Prayer was not possible, so I limited my remarks to God to bare civilities.

Next on the agenda was listening to tapes. I had with me cassette tapes of the Bible readings from the previous umpteen years of Keswick Conventions. Two hours of John Stott, Alec Motyer and Dick Lucas, and it was lunch time. After lunch I would set off for a long hike over the mountains. If there was a trace of depression in my system, then I was determined to walk it off and to let it blow away into the Atlantic Ocean. Finally, following an evening meal, I worked on the book I had started in Northumberland, the one Max's accident had interrupted. It gave me an outlet and a feeling of achievement. It is very disheartening to feel useless.

I don't know how useful that routine was, but I followed it religiously. The morning runs nearly finished me. I thought I might die of a heart attack at any moment, a thought which spurred me on to greater efforts. What a respectable way to go. 'Evangelist dies of heart attack while running in the Highlands.' At least then I would know the answer to the question, 'Is there a God?' But it would be embarrassing to arrive in uncertainty, so I moderated my efforts!

The Keswick tapes were heavy going. I really don't remember anything of what I heard, but then I have no recollection of anything I ate for my meals during that trip either, and presumably they nourished me.

The book never was finished, so my delusion of usefulness was as contrived as much of that which passes as Christian service.

The most useful part of the whole regime was the walking. It was borne in on me repeatedly that the natural beauty and order of things speaks with a quiet eloquence in a language which one can be attuned to when the written word has lost its attractiveness. It seems to restore one's soul without the need to expend any mental effort. Maybe that is what the 'green pastures' and 'still waters' did for King David.

On one of my afternoon rambles I set off for Greshornish Point. It was on another part of the island which I had not previously explored. I parked the car and headed down a promising trail. The promise proved false, the trail having been started by a sheep with no sense of commitment. So I stumbled on through the heather, bracken and rocks. Finally,

I came to the seashore, where the sheep or hikers had worn a definite path of sorts. Left or right was the choice, for straight on was a long drop to the sea below. I followed the path left, heading south.

It was a fabulous day in early October. The sun shone bright, the wind blew fresh, the waves responded in white caps which dashed their glee on the rocks. The oyster-catchers screamed their resentment of my intrusion, and the gulls swooped, dived and flirted with the wind. Occasionally a seal would show its head and gaze up at me with as much fascination as I returned. Then he would be away and about the business of catching his daily quota of fish.

By and by, it became apparent that the path I was following had grown into more than the random whims of foraging sheep. There were the rotting remains of bridges traversing the numerous streams which ran down from the hills to the sea. Someone must have had some purpose in travelling that route, for a stony foundation was still in evidence across areas of peat marsh and rocky obstructions had been laboriously attacked to clear passage.

So I followed the long-abandoned track, fascinated to discover its purpose. Soon it descended the cliffs to the water's edge and skirted a sandy bay which was full of the flotsam and jetsam of the sea. There were old fish boxes and lumps of polystyrene, Coca-Cola cans and torn fishing nets. The rotting ribs of an old boat protruded above the sand.

At the far end of the bay I left the random rejects of the sea to pursue the forgotten purpose of the old road. It zigzagged steeply up the mountain for a couple of hundred feet, then levelled off in a protected shelf of lush green grass. A stream ran by it, and a few weather-beaten trees maintained a sparse living.

It was obvious that this had been somebody's home. Generations had lived here till disaster or economic necessity had driven them away. There were old stone walls, the shells of two cottages now overgrown with ivy and bracken. I clambered through the ruins and wondered about those who had lived there. Were they fishers or farmers? I imagined children playing in the stream, and the mothers hanging out the washing to dry in the wind. They would have looked down there into the bay and seen the boats being beached at the close of the day's fishing. They could have looked across the bay and seen anyone who was approaching along the road I had just walked. Had that been the route along which the bearer of bad news had travelled, which had finally driven them from their peaceful haven? How blessed they must have been to have had no phones, no televisions, no motor cars to shatter their peace. I don't suppose they would have seen it in such a light, but it is easy to romanticise things with hindsight.

I sat down on the grass and leaned against the stone wall by the gap which must once have been a front door. What a trouble-free place to live – just the sort of habitation to which busy people dream of escaping. Yet trouble must have ousted the former inhabitants. Did they believe in God? Looking across the bay to the distant mountains beyond, it was difficult to see how any could do much other than believe in some kind of a creator. Yet here I sat, torn between the nagging demands of my doubts and a driving desire to believe.

Everything has a purpose, the mountains, the sea and the birds. The moment I became conscious of its existence, the remains of the track which had led me to this abandoned homestead had demanded a reason, a destination, a creator. Generations had walked it, so it must lead somewhere. I had followed it and discovered its secret. Generations had trodden the path of faith in God. That must count for something. It would be sheer arrogance to imagine that I, Justyn Rees, was the very first to discover that the promising road of faith in God, trodden for millennia, was in fact no better than the sheep trails which had led me astray earlier in the afternoon. Was there no God, no destination, no purpose? Were all those who had worn the trail heading nowhere?

Why were there no people still living here? The path they had once built had ceased to have relevance once home was uprooted by bad news. Was that why I was lost? Had bad news destroyed my security and safe home in God, thereby rendering the path of faith obsolete and increasingly obscure?

It was cold and the sun was sinking fast. This friendly place would soon become a haunt for uncertain fears as night replaced day. Instead of retracing my path along the sheep tracks, I resolved to follow the old road on the assumption that it must lead back to civilisation. Why couldn't it be as straightforward as that to find my way back to God?

As I followed the ancient trail I mulled over the confusing and often conflicting advice that had been given me, each intended to point me back to the right path:

'Justyn, you are too narrow. You need to get away from Hildenborough to broaden your horizons.'

'When the wind blows hard, send down deep roots and hang on for all you are worth. Don't make any changes.'

'You have had too much responsibility put on you too young. Get away and have some fun. Let your hair down!'

'When the ship is in danger, the captain must be seen on the bridge. This is the cost of leadership.'

'What you need is the baptism of the Holy Spirit.'

'You are too charismatic!'

'Hold on tight to the things you have been taught since childhood.'

'You are too spiritually minded for your own good. Get away and get your hands dirty in real living.'

'You are suffering from mid-life crisis. Be patient. It will pass.'

'You are suffering from depression. Take a break and the right medication.'

'You are concealing a hidden sin. If you won't obey God then you won't be able to believe in him, either.'

'You are stale. Make a change.'

'You are the object of satanic oppression. Trust God and stand firm.'

'You have lost your nerve! God has not given us the spirit of timidity. Trust in God!'

'You have come to the end of your own resources, you are burned out. Let go and let God.'

'You need to mature in your faith. Some of the things you have been seeking from God are the naive expectations of an adolescent Christian.'

'God is trying to tell you something. Listen!'

With all those diagnoses, I felt like a disorientated motorist seeking the right exit as he goes the wrong way round a traffic island. Poor Job must have suffered the same confusion at the hands of his advisers: '*You are worthless physicians, all of you! I have heard many things like these. How can you console me with your nonsense? Would a wise man answer with empty notions, with useless words, with speeches that have no value? Will your long-winded speeches never end? If only you would be altogether silent!'*

That's what I appreciated about being on Skye. There was no one to tell me what I should or should not do. Nevertheless, the words of my friends came back to haunt me. But what I really wanted was to meet with God. '*I desire to speak to the Almighty and to argue my case with God.*' That was why I had come to Skye.

How much simpler it was to follow that old Greshornish trail, which did indeed lead me right back to the very place I had left the car earlier that afternoon.

The day following my Greshornish hike, it rained. In Scotland, they say that if it is clear enough to see the mountains, it is a sure sign that it is about to rain. But if you cannot see the mountains, it means it is raining! That day you could hardly see the tree tops, let alone the mountains. The rain deluged my caravan on the outside and the windows misted up on the inside. The morning run was rained out, and the Keswick tapes were harder work than usual. A bad attack of cabin fever gripped me and a desire to scream was heavy upon me. So I resolved to go out for a cooked meal in civilisation.

I drove round in negligible visibility for some miles till I discerned through the gloom the magic sign 'Restaurant'. I followed the arrows down a side road till I came to a friendly little hotel with its slate roof pulled down over its ears for protection. It was situated right beside a jetty, and a short way over the water I could just perceive the outline of an island with a lighthouse on top.

I scurried into the hotel lobby and dripped on the carpet. A delicious smell wafted from the dining room, reassuring me that I was in the right place. A steaming bowl of soup, a roast chicken and an apple crumble later, I felt decidedly more human. I sat in the lounge, sipping coffee and enjoying the crackling fire. I noticed a display of Gavin Maxwell's books and decided to buy a copy of the sequel to *Ring of Bright Water*.

'Do you sell many of these?' I asked the kilted gentleman at the desk.

'Aye, we do that,' he replied.

'Do you know where Camus-Fèarna, Maxwell's old home is located?'

'There is no such place, but if you look from here over the water on a clear day, you'll see a white house on the shore. That is Sandaig, the real name for Camus-Fèarna.' I was fascinated.

'I recall from the book that at one stage Maxwell purchased an island just off Skye, almost opposite his home. If his Camus-Fèarna is just over the water, then the island can't be far from here. Do you happen to know where it is?'

'Aye, you're almost standing on it. It's the one with the lighthouse, just off the end of the jetty.'

'Does he still own it?'

'No, he sold it again. In any case, he's been dead some years so he'll not be needing property this side of the river.'

'Did you ever meet him?'

'Aye, he used to drop in often for a wee drink.'

Having purchased my book, I settled back with my coffee by the fire and was soon lost in the imaginary world of otters and lighthouses of Gavin Maxwell.

An hour or two later I awoke to the realisation that I had outstayed my welcome. The coffee was all gone and the bill was paid and the fire was past its prime. So I braced myself and headed for the door. But the bracing was unnecessary, for the rain had stopped and the sun was stabbing through the scurrying clouds. There in front of me was Maxwell's island lighthouse, and clearly visible over the water was the white house at Sandaig, the real Camus-Fèarna. The mist had rolled back, allowing the reality to replace the imaginary.

I wandered around in something of a daze, feeling like Alice having just stepped through the looking-glass. Up till then, this had all been a world of imagination and escapism. Now it was real.

Never far from my thoughts were the doubts, and soon they were horning in on the experience. There was the theory set out in the Bible. I had little problem accepting that. But the reality of day-to-day experience was another matter. I had enjoyed the escapism of an unreal world of faith and promise, but bridging the gap between faith and reality was not so easy. Maybe I was just unwilling to expose my hidden world to the harsher actualities of life on earth. It is one thing to believe the Bible when it says God answers prayer, but what happens when you need a cook for Hildenborough Hall? The promises that my God shall supply all your needs look good on paper, but what of financial deadlines which come and go with insufficient funds to meet their demands? The miracles of healing make heart-warming reading, but why hadn't Max been healed?

What happens when the mental picture you have derived from the description in the book doesn't correspond to the real place? Maybe there never was an otter. Maybe there never was a Gavin Maxwell. Maybe there never was a God. Yet I had talked to someone that very day who had claimed to know Maxwell. Maybe he just wanted to sell books. I had talked to many who had claimed to know God, had been one myself. Maybe we all just wanted to perpetuate religion or make believe an answer to our mysteries or take comfort in a mythical champion big enough to beat our fears.

Perhaps it was rather like the story of the atheist who went fishing on Loch Ness. Suddenly he felt a terrifying pull on his line, then a huge head broke the surface and a mouth full of menacing teeth rushed towards him. 'God help me!' screamed the atheist. 'But I thought you didn't believe in me,' came the unexpected reply. 'Yes, but I didn't believe in the Loch Ness Monster, either!'

I didn't read any more Maxwell after that, because it had ceased to be an escape and now demanded reconciliation with known reality.

The next day dawned noncommittally. It was dark and gloomy, though not actually raining. 'It is Saturday,' I rationalised, and decided to forgo the run. I went for a morning walk instead.

I made the mistake of trying to pray. The mistake was not so much in the praying as in the trying. I concentrated too hard and thought about what I was saying and who I was saying it to.

It is hard to identify it now, but I felt it definitely on that occasion, as on many others. I rarely feel it now, but I recall it as a cross between pain and nausea. Whenever my thoughts strayed into a certain area it was like touching an electric fence. I guess the mind put it there to warn me off. But I couldn't leave it, because my treasure was hidden there.

It was when I found myself longing to know God more than anything else in life, when I reached out to him and touched nothing; it was then that I would reel back in pain, struck in the face by a two-by-four called 'reality'. 'There is no God. It is just wishful thinking. The more you want him, the more you are in danger of fooling yourself into believing something which just is not true.'

Soon I quit praying and started thinking. The wind burrowed through the bracken and frisked the heather on up the mountainside. A few spots of rain stung my cheeks. A startled sheep scurried away, pursued by an overgrown youngster seeking nourishment and reassurance from its long-suffering mother's milk.

So there was no God. It was no good pursuing the matter. The sooner I faced up to the facts the better. I had come up here to find him and he was nowhere to be found, therefore he was not. I think the Russians once drew a similar conclusion from their space explorations.

'If there is no God, then how am I to live? My livelihood has been to preach. I must seek a new career. Perhaps I will go back to commercial flying. Then there are the children. How will I bring them up? Will I send them to church? What moral standards will I set for them? What will Joy do? Will she stay with me when her belief in the Bible would lead her not to be unequally yoked to an unbeliever? We will need to make a whole new circle of friends, irreligious friends.'

Then the two-by-four caught me on the back swing. I could no more contemplate the consequences of not believing than I could go on trying to regain my faith. Back and forth swung the two-by-four, bludgeoning my poor brain with every pass. The cost of believing seemed evenly balanced by the cost of not believing.

Rational thought was too painful. How simple it must have been for the Children of Israel at the foot of Sinai. With the mountain shaking and billowing fire and smoke in the presence of God, they could have been left in no doubt of his reality. Elijah had also stood on a mountain facing a crowd of sceptics. '*How long will you continue to limp between two different opinions?*' Their response had been as noncommittal as my own agnostic thoughts. But God had made it all so easy. The debate had ended with a unanimous vote in his favour, for God had settled the argument by a bolt of lightning.

I had reached the summit of the hill up which I had been labouring for some time. The tops of the mountains over the water were obscured with the lowering clouds. The sea below me was a boiling churn of frenzied water. The ever freshening wind blasted the salty air in my face. The few tenacious shrubs and heather clung precariously to the rocky soil as they were shaken by the onslaught. One stubborn tree slanted at forty-five degrees twenty feet from where I stood.

I fell to my knees in the heather. I wanted satisfaction.

'God, if you hear me, I desperately need to know if you are there. Please let me know it right now. I cannot find the answer within my own human capacity to reason, but if you are there and if you care at all, please send down fire from Heaven and consume that tree.'

Nothing happened.

I waited. Still nothing. Job's frustration was mine: '*I cry out to you, O God, but you do not answer; I stand up, but merely look at me. Oh, that I had someone to hear me! Why do you hide your face?'*

No response, nothing but the howling wind. *'Will you torment a windblown leaf?'*

At last I went back to the caravan and, lying down on the bunk, sought oblivion in sleep.

It was the shaking of the van which woke me in the middle of the afternoon. The wind was blowing with unusual force. I brewed coffee and staggered out to drink it sitting on a rock. The tide was higher than I had ever seen it and the waves were dramatic. I took a walk around the bay and watched the Atlantic vent its fury against the Castle of Doon. Gouts of spray flecked the evening sunlight, and as I rounded a rock, I was nearly knocked to the ground by the full force of the wind. It was magnificent and terrifying.

'Beware of the equinoctial gales,' I had been warned. I hurried back to secure the van and hitched it up to the car. I put rocks on the skylights and double-checked every window latch.

The light began to fade and I wondered if there were such things as ghosts. I knew several people who claimed to have seen strange sights and heard unaccountable voices. There was the friend who had seen the outline of a woman with her hair blowing in the wind, standing on a clifftop looking out to sea. The old lady who heard footsteps coming up her stairs to her bedroom door at night. The picnickers who had heard a woman's voice singing by a stream. The man who had heard the noise of an army marching along a road where no road existed. The Highlands abound with such tales. But then if you don't believe in God, why believe in ghosts? On the other hand, if you have no set ideas on truth, then just about anything could be true.

Job had evidently believed in ghosts and the phantoms of his imagination had only added to his discomfort:

Amid disquieting dreams in the night, when deep sleep falls on men, fear and trembling seized me and made all my bones shake. A spirit glided past my face, and the hair on my body stood on end. It stopped, but I could not tell what it was. A form stood before my eyes, and I heard a hushed voice: 'Can a mortal be more righteous than God? Can a man be more pure than his Maker?'

If Job believed in ghosts then they must exist, but then Job had believed in God also. I argued it back and forth and scurried into the van to light a candle to dispel the shadows, just in case!

The rain started and the wind blew stronger and the night closed in.

I was shut up in an isolated world of my own with no God to turn to and no one I loved even knew my whereabouts. Maybe this night I would just blow away and no one would ever know.

I didn't blow away, but in the early hours of the morning the storm blew itself out and I eventually found sleep.

Sunday morning was relatively calm. 'The Sabbath is a day of rest' excused the run for a third day in succession. Now what should I do about church? I hadn't resolved that one, so I yielded to a lifetime of habit and went. It was important to find a service in English, the Gaelic not being one of my strong points. At Kyleakin I found a church with promise and took my place in the prevailing silence. The long-faced minister mounted the pulpit and the congregation rose.

The reading was from Psalm 42. '*As the deer pants for streams of water, so my soul pants for you, O God. My soul thirsts for God, for the living God. When can I go and meet with God? My tears have been my food day and night, while men say to me all day long, "Where is your God?"* '

I thought of the two-by-four and wondered if the writer of this psalm had experienced its punishment.

The psalm continued: '*These things I remember as I pour out my soul: how I used to go with the multitude, leading the procession to the house of God, with shouts of joy and thanksgiving among the festive throng.*'

A mental picture of the chapel of Hildenborough Hall came to mind. There I was, leading the multitude in the house of God and feeling a fraud. Surely the psalmist could never have felt that way.

'*Why are you downcast, O my soul? Why so disturbed within me? Put your hope in God, for I will yet praise him, my Saviour and my God.*'

So maybe he had felt as I did. And maybe there was a hope of getting over it.

Then came the sermon. Apparently this was part of a series on the book of Job. 'Cheerful stuff,' I thought. 'Just what I need to cheer me up!'

'Today we will consider what was probably the greatest of Job's trials,' purred the soft Highland accent. 'The trial I refer to is Job's loss of the sense of the presence of God.' I was wide awake and listening.

'I read from the twenty-third chapter of the book of Job: "*Behold I go forward, but he is not there: and backward, but I cannot perceive him; on the left hand I seek him, but I cannot behold him; I turn to the right hand, but I cannot see him . . . But he knows the way that I take and when he has tried me, I shall come forth as gold."* '

I don't recall the details of the talk but I know that he likened Job's horrifying sense of aloneness to that of Jesus on the cross, when he cried out in anguish, 'My God, my God, why have you forsaken me?'

The last hymn finished me and I was unable to fight back the tears as the congregation sang:

> Be still my soul, the Lord is on your side.
> Bear patiently the cross of grief or pain.
> Leave to thy God to order and provide;
> In every change He faithful will remain . . .
> Thy hope, thy confidence let nothing shake;
> All now mysterious shall be bright at last.

I left my seat and fled for the door before the hymn was done, conscious of the amazed looks of the congregation, for whom emotion had no place in religion.

I walked on the beach. 'Though I cannot find him, yet he knows the way that I take. His intention is to try me that I may come forth as gold. If the psalmist felt downcast in his soul, if Job and even Jesus knew what it was to lose the sense of the presence of God, and if the hymn writer could so exactly reflect my feelings, then I am not alone. There is hope.'

'God,' I prayed, ducking the two-by-four, 'I may not be able to find you, but thank you that you have not lost me. Please hold on tight and don't let me go.'

Next day I headed home. I had failed in my mission to find God, but I had a degree of peace in the thought that perhaps he had not lost me.

10

Faith is Not the Point

When I got home Hildenborough was quiet as a tomb.
There were no guests or staff, just a big, empty, echoing
house. There wasn't much to be done either, so I took to
accompanying Max on his speaking engagements. He was
receiving an ever increasing flow of invitations to share his
experiences and was glad to have a chauffeur to drive him
around. I fear my company was of questionable benefit to
one in need of cheer. By and by I could give Max's talk as
well as he could. In a weak moment I suggested that I
should limp into one of his meetings and give his testimony,
as though I were Max, the recovering paraplegic. His
Christian ethics were still intact, so he wouldn't let me.

Maybe it was frustration at being unable to contribute
anything more than driving ability, or maybe it was the
weather, but one grey afternoon while driving home over
Salisbury Plain I let fly at Max a long destructive tirade
about the unreality of the Christian faith.

'Has it ever occurred to you, Max, that faith may just be
an extension of the imagination? Imagination when inspired
by fear can lead people to believe they see things that are
not there and can make them act in irrational, destructive
ways. Take the Druids who used to worship here on
Salisbury Plain as a perfect example. Who knows what

horrors went on at Stonehenge? And why? It was just their imaginations playing tricks on them. So could it not then be equally possible that imagination might also lead people to believe that they see good things that are not there, and so cause them to behave in a positive way?'

'I see imagination as an entirely neutral thing, like a TV. You can use it for good or bad. *"Faith is being sure of what we hope for and certain of what we do not see"* – that sounds like imagination to me. Imagination can conjure things that are unreal, or it can recall memories of reality, much as a photographer might do.'

'So what do you do with the Druids and their sincerely held beliefs? And what of all the people who continue to worship demons and devils and perpetrate all manner of crimes in their names?'

'But Jay, don't you agree that such practices are self-condemning? Whether or not the entities they worship are the products of their imagining, their consequent behaviour writes off their beliefs as not right. But the other side of the coin is that believing in God causes people to behave in a very right manner. It makes them kind, peaceful, generous, honest.'

'OK. Point taken, but what about all the good things people do, inspired by questionable realities that they claim to have seen.'

'Such as?'

'Weeping statues of Mary, perhaps even some of the things I saw in Tunbridge Wells back in the spring. Just because they inspire people positively doesn't make them real.'

'If you ask me, Jay, God is much bigger-minded than most theologians. He is not so hung up on correct protocol as we are.'

'What are you getting at?'

'Well, take the wise men who came to worship Jesus in Bethlehem. How did they find their way?'

'They followed the star.'

'That sounds like astrology to me, and what self-respecting evangelical theologian would condone astrology? We'd be swapping Bible-reading notes for horoscopes in no time! No, I think God is big-minded and will use all kinds of things, some real and some imagined, to increase our faith. What if some of those things are only the products of our imagination? It only goes to underscore the grace of God. It does not render God unreal.'

'Did you know Job believed in ghosts?' I popped in.

'What makes you think that, Jay?'

I quoted the passage that had disturbed me back on Skye.

'Have you read much of Job recently?'

'Yes, I have. It's quite an encouragement to see that I am not alone.'

'You should keep reading Job. It has a happy ending!'

'Ah, happy endings! "They all lived happily ever after!" Sounds like a fair story to me!'

We pulled into a service station to fill the tank. Being more agile than Max, I jumped out and held the nozzle. Max wound down the window.

'You know, Jay, you may not be able to believe, but I do believe. I am sure that God does love you and his love will never let go of you. You can doubt all you like, but I know that God will never be unfaithful to you. I believe for you.'

I dare say that was the most significant thing anyone ever said to me. I couldn't argue, for I was filling the tank.

But neither did I want to argue. For the first time in months I felt a spark of assurance. Something had got through to my heart.

As we drove off: 'But I am vulnerable, Max. If faith is my shield then I have dropped it. I have no faith and therefore am defenceless.'

'Yes, but I will hold up the shield for you. And in any case, faith is not your defence, but God is. It is his faithfulness which acts as a shield to protect you, not your faith. King David knew that: "*The Lord is my fortress, my deliverer, my rock, my shield, my stronghold, my refuge and my saviour.*" Your faith only affects the way you feel, but in fact you are perfectly safe in his protection. You may feel secure or you may feel vulnerable, at peace or in turmoil, but either way the fact remains that behind the protection of God you are utterly and unconditionally safe.'

'Are you saying, then, that faith is just a feeling?'

'Forget faith, Justyn! That's not what I am talking about. What counts is not your faith, but rather God's faithfulness. "*I have loved you with an everlasting love; therefore I have continued faithfulness to you ... If we are faithless, he remains faithful – for he cannot deny himself.*" '

It wasn't just the words. Max himself seemed to put flesh on to the meaning by being to me a very convincing representation of Jesus. If Max cared enough about me to continue to hold up my shield of protection despite my faithlessness, how much more would Jesus do so – if there really was a Jesus, that is.

The ancient ring of stones stood stark against the grey sky as we drove past Stonehenge. The clouds hung low and the wind flung the rain across the dreary landscape. Those stones had stood against the onslaught of thirty-eight centuries of erosion, yet there they were, unaffected by the elements.

'Some things never change,' I commented. 'The fellows who dragged those stones here all the way from Wales must have seen the surrounding countryside much as it still is.'

'They would have had quite a shock to see us whizzing by!' returned Max, ruining the mood. 'But think of it this way, Justyn. Your feelings of faith are as capricious as the clouds, but God is as safe and unchangeable as these ancient stones. I bet that is exactly what David thought as he crouched behind a rock, sheltering from a storm. *"He who dwells in the shelter of the Most High will rest in the shadow of the Almighty. I will say of the Lord, 'He is my refuge and my fortress, my God, in whom I trust.'"* '

For a few miles we drove in silence. I was turning over in my mind the revolutionary thought that it was not so important that I should believe in God, but that God should believe in me. Perhaps I could rest in the reality that if God were God, then he would remain faithful to me despite my unfaithfulness. Somehow that thought removed the stress from the situation. I no longer needed to fear the consequences of my doubts, nor need I fret over a solution to them. I could leave it in the hands of the God who might be there and Max who definitely was there and was convinced that God was also.

The thought did much to cheer me, so our conversation turned to more earthly matters.

'Why don't we go on a trip to America? You can preach and I will carry your bags. I am sure Peter Letchford would arrange an itinerary for you. And besides, he might be able to help me get straightened out.' And so we planned the trip.

* * *

Just four weeks later we boarded a flight to New York in search of the New World. We made our base with Peter and Dorothy Letchford, who were running a thriving church in upper New York State. Peter had been a life-long friend of my father. We consumed gallons of ice cream and Max gave his talk till I found myself muttering bits of it in my sleep.

Peter put aside as much time as he could and I bombarded him with questions in an attempt to get solutions. We walked and talked in the cemetery. That place had special memories for me. I had walked there with my father nine years previously. Maybe in talking with Peter I was subconsciously seeking an interview with my father. Doubtless that is the conclusion psychiatrists would have drawn. Either way, I was disappointed. I had come a long way and my hopes had been raised with every mile. But Peter had no magic formula to offer. He was kind and sympathetic, but he didn't solve the problem. I was no further ahead. But we laughed a lot, and laughter offers its own kind of medicine.

'I hope you don't mind, Justyn,' said Peter after we had been there for a few days, 'but I have taken the liberty of phoning Stephen Olford in Florida to tell him of your problems.' Stephen Olford was another life-long friend of the family and a fiery preacher. Maybe I could get the paternal advice I sought from him. Father had been staying at his home, then in New York City, when he had died eight years previously.

'He has invited you to fly down to spend a day with him.' I thought that was a grand idea, so readily agreed. Max was going to Washington to visit a girl called Joni

Eriksen who had suffered a similar accident to his own. She had recently published a book about her experiences, so Max was keen to pick her brains. Maybe he'd get some fresh inspiration for his own talk which might change it a little! In any case I could leave him to his own devices for thirty-six hours.

'Stephen would like you to visit a psychiatrist friend in New York before you go.' I was not at all sure that I liked that part of the bargain. A psychiatrist! What in the world would I do with one of those? So I told Max what was in the wind, expecting him to laugh the idea out of court. To my consternation, he didn't.

'You don't think I'm losing my marbles, do you?' I asked anxiously.

'No, I don't. But depression is one diagnosis you have not seriously considered. If I were you I would leave no stone unturned.'

I went to visit Dr Angus Foulks in one of those topless New York buildings. I don't love New York, whatever the slogans may say. It has about it a sense of evil and suffocation. It was there that my father had died, and I could imagine no good thing coming from such a city. I supposed that if you have to do something as unpleasant as seeing a psychiatrist, then a more sympathetic place to do it than New York would be hard to find.

I waited in an ante room pretending to read a magazine. 'I wonder if he's watching me even now through a secret window. I must play it cool. If he knows how terrified I feel he'll have me in a straitjacket quick as a flash.'

Dr Foulks was a very nice, very ordinary fellow. I suppose he did interview me, but I can't say I noticed. I never did lie on a couch or enter a hypnotic trance. When the hour was over I asked him about making another appointment so he could start the examination. I was most surprised to discover that he had already reached his diagnosis. He was satisfied that I was suffering from clinical depression. 'It is a kind of chemical imbalance which affects the brain,' he told me.

'Now how in the world could he so quickly reach that conclusion – and without any kind of examination?' I asked myself, fighting for survival through the New York traffic as it jostled up Broadway and left on to 57th Street. 'Could my loss of faith really be put down to an imbalance of chemicals? If Dr Foulks is right, then is faith just a right chemical balance? Doesn't the Bible teach that faith comes by hearing and hearing by the word of God? But if faith comes by a correct balance of chemicals, then Paul should have written that into the tenth chapter of Romans.

'But just supposing Dr Foulkes is right. Supposing I am depressed, which is the cause of which? Am I depressed because I have lost my faith, or have I lost my faith because I am depressed?'

It seemed that everyone I talked to tended to diagnose the problem according to his own sphere of expertise. To a preacher it was a spiritual problem. To a doctor it was depression. If you label things according to what you understand, then I guess it makes you feel secure in the knowledge that you are in control, you have it filed in the right pigeon-hole.

By now I had broken free from the congestion of 57th Street and was heading north on the Henry Hudson Parkway.

'If a surgeon were to open up my body in search of faith, I wonder where he would look,' I pondered. 'I suppose my head is as good a place as any. It is my brain which stores and processes information. If faith is a response to facts, then presumably it is part of the processing of information. I can understand how an imbalance of chemicals could upset my brain. But is my faith as vulnerable as my brain? If a person, for whatever reason, loses his mind, does he also lose his faith, and with it his relationship with God? Pop's brain was all messed up by the tumour, yet I recall that he could pray clearly even when he couldn't speak clearly.'

The George Washington Bridge was coming up on the left and my map suggested that if I crossed it I could pick up the Palisades Interstate north.

'It's not hard to believe in this bridge, and there seems no struggle of the will to decide whether or not to follow the information suggested by my map. My chemical imbalance doesn't seem to be attacking that aspect of my decision-making ability. Maybe it's because my will isn't affected, whereas believing in God is more a choice of my will.

'So faith must have more to do with my will than my intellect. If my intellect is in my head and can be examined by psychiatrists, where is my will? And who is qualified to examine it and diagnose a malfunction?'

I paid my toll and turned north, watching the Hudson river slip by on my right.

'I wonder, then, if I haven't chosen to doubt, as an act of my will? Maybe to doubt has become an attractive option as a let-out from the cost of going on believing. I don't think I have consciously made that decision, but the aggravation of going on trusting God for all the needs of Hildenborough has been a terrible burden. In any case, if I have chosen to doubt then I did so with my will. I was not forced into doubting by an imbalanced chemistry.'

Undoubtedly to lose my faith was the most depressing experience of my life. But to admit that depression was the cause of it was quite another matter. Yet of all the diagnoses that others have attached to my doubts, depression is still the chief. As a diagnosis, that has its attractions, because to blame doubt on depression lifts the responsibility from my shoulders. 'I can't help it, you see. I am depressed, suffering from a chemical imbalance.' That way I am the victim of doubt, not the perpetrator.

I think the reason that other Christians prefer to blame my doubts on depression has to do with their own sense of security. To admit that it is possible for a Christian in his right mind to lose his faith is unsettling. 'If Justyn could lose his faith, then maybe I could.' But 'if Justyn was depressed and so lost his faith, then I am OK. Such "illness" is understandable. He lost his faith while the balance of his mind was impaired.' The sentence is reduced from eternal Hell to a course of treatment in a hospital!

As I drove north on Interstate 87 it began to dawn on me that the cost of believing was outweighed by the cost of not believing. Being 'faithful unto death' sounds heavy, but being unfaithful unto separation from God is heavier. Until I faced that option, infidelity had all the advantages. Doubting had offered me an attractive let-out, a way of escape. But the escape also had unforeseen disadvantages, which were, perhaps, bigger than the disadvantages of believing.

'So what is my choice?' I questioned myself. 'Would I rather trust God, or would I rather doubt him? No contest. I want to trust God. But I cannot trust God if I don't believe in his existence.'

And there was the big question. Was my chemically imbalanced brain making it impossible to believe in God, or at any rate to choose to trust him? Or had my unconscious choice not to trust God triggered an imbalance in my chemistry, rendering me incapable of believing in God's existence? A vicious circle.

Paul taught that it is '*by open statement of the truth that we commend ourselves to every man's conscience*'. So he addressed the conscience when seeking to encourage men to believe. He didn't address the intellect.

'*You will seek me and find me when you seek me with all your heart.*' Jeremiah must have had a similar idea, for he taught that God is to be found by the one who employs the heart. How do we know God? By faith. Where is faith? Presumably in the heart, for '*man believes with his heart*' . . .

So if someone wants to encourage your faith he addresses your conscience. If your conscience prompts you to respond, it will be with your heart that you will seek God. And if you are successful in your search it will be with your heart that you will believe. And ultimately, if you learn to love God, you will do so with all your heart, which will affect your mind, soul and physical body – perhaps even your chemistry, though Moses didn't add that to the list.

'*What do you want me to do for you?*' Jesus asked blind Bartimaeus. Well, he didn't need omniscience to be able to figure out what was wrong with the man. So perhaps Jesus just wanted to hear his reply – '*I want to see.*'

Jesus never asked him if he believed. He just told him: '*Go your way; your faith has made you well.*'

Just how did Jesus know that he believed? Who had said

anything about faith? There must have been a direct link between the man's will and his faith. For the man to express his will in the matter was for him to express his faith in the matter.

And where does hope come in? '*Faith is being sure of what we hope for . . .*' Perhaps the blind man's wish – '*I want to see*' – was more an expression of hope than of faith. So perhaps it would be more beneficial for me to quest for hope than for faith. After all, hope is the destination while faith is but the means to get there.

'*Where your treasure is, there shall your heart be also.*' Jesus said that, so it was a reliable lead. 'One man's meat is another man's poison.' Jesus didn't say that, yet the truth is evident that one man's idea of treasure, what he considers valuable, may leave another man cold. Treasure is treasure simply because a man chooses to value it. Finding it becomes his hope, his life-long search. But another man's choice rejects it as worthless so he doesn't seek it because he doesn't hope for it.

God is a treasure to some; others reject him as worthless.

By the time I had jumped through all these theological hoops I was halfway to Albany. The daylight was fading, so I stopped to revive myself with a cup of caffeine and an English muffin.

'I wonder if I have become half-hearted in my search for God and if that could be to blame for my doubting him. I was wholehearted when first I sought him, but maybe other things have crept in which I have also treated as treasure. But what? Broughton Manor? Perhaps my preaching ministry? But these are things which God has promised. It was he who put them into my life, so why should he be upset if I take them to heart? Could it be that they have become more important to me than God himself? "If I don't get that house and if you don't use me as a preacher, then I don't want to know you. You are only useful to me for what I can get out of you. Failure to come up with the goods renders you useless, unattractive and consequently unbelievable. What is the sense of praying in faith if you don't deliver?" '

Was I double-minded, as James had described the doubter? Was I undecided, with my will set on more than one choice and my heart seeking after more than one treasure? If so, perhaps that explained my doubts. But the heart is deceitful above all things, and to search it and know it is beyond human scrutiny, especially when the brain you seek to employ in the search is suffering from a chemical imbalance!

When eventually I got back to the Letchfords' home I had a head full of new thoughts to share with Max. I don't think he bought my new revelations. Dr Foulks was much more believable. My chemistry needed a re-tune.

Next day I flew to Florida. The amazing December heat hit me as I stepped off the plane. And there was I in a world of sprinklers and reed grass, palm trees, air conditioners and the constant purr of crickets. Joy and I had lived there for six months when we were first married while I had undertaken an intensive course in commercial flying. It felt good to be back.

Stephen Olford was tied up when I arrived so I took a walk along the seashore. Bradenton Beach was a far cry from the Isle of Skye. The waters of the Gulf of Mexico were warm and inviting. The sand was bleached white. The trees were palms and stood upright, rather than the wind-blasted, forty-five-degree pines of the Western Isles. The sun set over the Gulf, spilling purple and orange over the surface of the water.

How simple things had been when we had lived there before; no Hildenborough Hall to run, all four of our parents alive and healthy, no one we knew had a broken neck. The world had been before us with no backlog of disappointments to limit our horizons. We could trust God for anything, for what had we ever lacked? Even the sky was no limit to what we could hope to accomplish.

But in the intervening years problems had crowded in. For a while naive optimism had kept me going. I was young and life was before me. There was no such thing as a problem to which a solution could not be found. There was bound to be some avenue that I had yet to consider around any difficulty that arose.

But then some problems had remained unsolved, compounding, the one upon the other, in a log-jam across my hope for the future. The sky was no longer the limit; the log-jam was.

Was I suffering from mid-life crisis? Was this just the transition from youth to maturity?

'Hello, Justyn. How absolutely super to see you,' beamed Stephen and Heather Olford as I arrived at their home.

They took me out to a lovely meal that evening, then we talked. I poured out my heart once again. I was getting good at it now, and the facts flowed as freely as Max's story! 'Could I be suffering from mid-life crisis?'

'You hardly seem old enough for that! But maybe you are experiencing something of the spiritual equivalent. You see, trusting God is not just one of several options. It can only ever be unique. Proverbs tells us to trust in the

Lord with all our heart, not dividing our heart between leaning on God and leaning on our own understanding. Jeremiah goes so far as to pronounce a curse on anyone who trusts in man and flesh, thereby diverting his heart from God. The worried father who brought his demon-possessed boy to Jesus was rebuked when he asked, "If you can do anything, have pity on us and help us." "If I can?" Jesus retorted, "if I can?" Evidently Jesus was not impressed with the kind of approach to him that was but one of several options.

'Maybe, Justyn, you have subconsciously been approaching Jesus with the same kind of attitude. "Lord, if you can do anything, have pity on me and help me. But I am young and may well still be able to find a solution in some area I have not yet tried. I wouldn't want you to think that I am in a real bind. Your help would be greatly appreciated, but if you can't help then I'll find some other way round this."

'Real faith has no back doors, no other possibilities, no alternates. It could be that God has brought you to a place of spiritual mid-life crisis, a road block which only God himself can get you through.'

Next morning, over breakfast, we talked some more. Between orange juice and muffins, we caught the eight o'clock news on the television. There was an item about a new church being built in California, all of glass. Robert Schuller still needed four million dollars to complete the project. When asked by the interviewer if he was confident of raising such a sum, he replied, 'This church will be a demonstration of the power of "Possibility Thinking". I am convinced that the money will be available as each dollar is needed.'

'Do you know Schuller?' I asked my host, as the picture vanished.

'Yes, I have met him.'

'Well, is he kosher?'

'I believe so.'

'If you ask me, I think he is a humbug. With confidence like that he will raise the money whether or not there is a God to supply all his needs. He doesn't need God when he has a faith as strong as that. His faith is all he really needs to get him through. For him, "Possibility Thinking" has become a substitute for God. That's just what I mean. To lose your self-confidence is for God to vanish off the scene. "Faith" is all there is to it. The genuine existence of God has nothing to do with it.' I think the Olfords were a little startled at my outburst. The vehemence of it surprised me, too.

So we launched into a lengthy discussion on the relationship between the reality of God and faith. I told them what Max had emphasised on Salisbury Plain, how he had stressed that faith was nothing in itself, but that God's faithfulness was everything. We talked all morning, till it was time for me to catch the flight back to the frozen north. As we drove to the airport, I noticed the abundance of motor homes, huge vehicles as big as buses. What fun it would be to bring the whole family over for a trip in one of those. 'Possibility Thinking'?

I climbed aboard the plane somewhat disappointed that once again I had drawn a blank. Stephen Olford had offered much that was helpful by way of advice, but he had not taken the doubts away. I was no nearer to a solution. What I was seeking was power to believe, not advice on how belief might be achieved or more diagnoses on why I didn't believe.

I buckled myself into the seat as instructed. '*Be still, my soul, the Lord is on your side.*' The engines started to moan. Was faith just 'Possibility Thinking'? Surely there had to be more to it than the correct balance of chemicals in the brain. The one-eleven taxied to the active runway. Where could I find the power to believe? 'Forget faith, Justyn! That's not what I am talking about. What counts is not your faith, but rather God's faithfulness.' The plane was lined up with the centre line, ready for take-off. A flood of memories came to me. I had taken off from that very runway dozens of times during my commercial pilot's training. I was a bad back-seat driver now that I was not at the controls, and I felt a strange tinge of nervousness. I had lost my faith and was not at the controls of my walk with God, either.

The moan crescendoed to a scream. Would 'Possibility Thinking' get us off the ground? '*I have loved you with an everlasting love; therefore I have continued faithfulness to you . . . If we are faithless, he remains faithful – for he cannot deny himself.*'

The brakes were released and a surge of power thrust me back into the seat. 'You may not be able to believe, but I do believe. I am sure that God does love you and his love will never let go of you. You can doubt all you like, but I know that God will never be unfaithful to you. I believe for you.'

We were airborne and I had had nothing whatever to do with it. It had in no way been dependent on my faith, nor had my doubts jeopardised it. 'Possibility Thinking' could never have achieved it!

I would rest in God, rather than striving to regain my faith. I doubted my faith, and I even doubted my doubts. But in God's faithfulness I was prepared to rest.

The Florida landscape spread out like a map below us. I

was conscious of the insistent voice of a stewardess asking me if I wanted a drink. I couldn't turn from the window, for tears were streaming down my cheeks – tears of relief. Just for an instant I had experienced a flash of rest – soul peace.

I got back to the Letchfords' home in Albany within an hour of Max. He was full of his time with Joni Eriksen. 'It's amazing what similarities there are between her story and mine.'

'Then I don't want to hear it! I've heard it so many times before.'

But nothing could kill Max's enthusiasm. 'I'm going to write a book. I've got the outline down already. It came to me on the plane.' Apparently air travel was a source of great inspiration that day! Eventually he asked: 'Oh, and how was your trip?'

'Remember our conversation last month as we drove past Stonehenge? Well, the truth of what you were saying is starting to get into my heart. My doubts are still there, but I have a new sense of hope.'

There was a letter waiting for me from Dr Foulks. He recommended that a complete change and a rest would be the best cure for my clinical depression. Why fight the diagnosis when the prescribed cure was so palatable? Besides, I had an idea.

Next day I took Max to check out the prices of those motor homes I had seen in Florida.

11

A Nature Walk

'You must be joking!' Joy looked at me as if I were out of my mind. I was getting used to that look, so I never flinched. 'Three weeks to move out of our house, pack for three months away and prepare ourselves and the children for a North American safari, and all that over Christmas and New Year?'

I had done some checking as soon as we had arrived home. Motor homes in England were twice the price of those I had seen in Florida. Even allowing for the cost of shipping, there should be a possibility of our buying such a vehicle in the US, living in it for a few months and then bringing it back to resell in England. We might even get our money back.

Joy, the realist, was dubious about the financial possibilities, but was quick to recognise the value of an extended time away. We immediately put the house on the market, and to our amazement sold it by lunchtime on the very first day it was advertised. Joy was convinced. Cash in the bank was a powerful argument.

The children didn't need much persuasion to take a term out of school, though their headmistress despised the plan as 'educationally unsound'. So we didn't ask her gracious permission; we just told her we were going.

One month after leaving the Letchfords, we were back with them in Albany, New York. And three days of wheeling and dealing later, we had purchased twenty-six feet of decadent luxury on wheels. Every conceivable comfort was included to turn the hardships of camping into the comforts of home. There was a fridge, a deep freeze, central heating, air conditioning, running hot and cold water, a shower, a flush toilet, a built-in stereo, a generator and a luxury interior. In fact, it was very much more comfortable than home, if a little smaller.

The children were in raptures. Even Joy was amazed. After six weeks of the previous summer in our tiny trailer, the prospect of three months' camping had not been an attractive proposition. But this was a different matter.

That night we pored over maps on the Letchfords' dining table. The snow drifting down outside caused our eyes to stray to the south. Florida. Sunshine. 'We've been there and it's flat and once you've seen one palm tree, you've seen them all.'

'How about southern California?' suggested Peter. 'You can be sure of sunshine over there, and it's not flat. You could drive across the southern states and avoid the worst of the winter weather.' He traced a line across the map from top right, where we were, to bottom left, where San Diego was marked, just north of Mexico. 'I know some folk there who could help you find a place to park the Winnebago.' San Diego sounded attractive, so next day we were off, like Columbus, to discover a new world.

It didn't take long to settle to the routine of being gypsies. Becky, being the smallest, had the top bunk. We had to wedge her in with cushions to make sure she didn't roll out in the night. 'That's enough!' she would squeak in near suffocation. Esther had the pull-down bunk over the driver's section, while Dan slept on the kitchen table, suitably padded for his comfort. Dan had never had any trouble sleeping and could drop off as easily on a kitchen table as he could on a feather bed.

We visited Joy's cousin in Philadelphia, friends in Chattanooga, Tennessee, and an ex-Hildenborough staff member in Tulsa, Oklahoma, then on west through Amarillo and Albuquerque towards the Grand Canyon.

Driving the motor home was a snap. My previous experience with Hildenborough's bus stood me in good shape. Cruise control! What a fine innovation, one rarely available on British vehicles. But then British vehicles seldom have the opportunity to cruise, being forced to spend the greater part of their time clogged in traffic congestion. But our new motor home was equipped with this most useful of buttons, the depressing of which relieved me of the necessity to co-ordinate the accelerator pedal with the speedometer. For mile after mile all I had to do was steer – no great feat, for the roads were wide, straight and empty. For hours, then days, I just sat there, watching the southern states glide by. There was little need to consult the map, for the same Interstate 40 would lead us all the way from Tennessee to California.

So speed and direction ceased to be of concern. Wherever the road took us, we would arrive whenever the cruise control decreed it. I didn't have to ask any questions. There were no decisions to be made. There were no doubts to be surmounted.

How was it that I couldn't live my life that way? Why should trusting God so severely add to the burden of living? 'You must believe!' – a crushing obligation placed on me by my religion. 'I don't want to live like that any longer,' I thought to myself. 'If God is real then it is he who made the road ahead, he who drew the map and it is he who sets the pace. If my faith led me to relax into such a confidence, then believing would cease to be a burden and become a release. Faith should be a matter of entering into his rest, not stressing myself into an early grave.'

I prayed occasionally, but only when the urge took me. I didn't deliberately make time to pray. And my praying was not asking. It was muttered observations that could have been mistaken for soliloquy. After all, if God was not real then all prayer was simply talking to yourself. I didn't bother to analyse the difference. But I did take time to read the Bible as a regular discipline. Job still offered the most sympathetic of themes, so I reread it and found myself identifying with that poor man's indignity at the hands of his friends, doubtless inspired by Satan, all by divine permission. If God is just, why does he permit injustice to prevail? Could that not be deemed negligence and therefore render God culpable?

A nagging thought constantly troubled me. It was a foolish thought now that I recall it, but it was a constant irritant. All those towns, each looking much the same as another, all full of households of people going about their daily lives thinking that their house was the centre of the world. They might scurry off to the post office, the bank, the grocery store, the office; but back they would return to the centre of their universe – home. And they did all that with no reference to me! I never knew they existed until I drove past and caught a glimpse of them on the sidewalk. Their whole town might cease to exist, and its demise would affect my life less significantly than a missed meal or a spilled cup of coffee. They didn't matter to me nor I to them. Their whole lives were merely wallpaper for my drive across America.

Might God think of them in the same way, or was it possible that each one found significance in his eyes? And if they did, what difference did it make to them? Were they happier, more fulfilled, more morally responsible?

We stopped one day in one of those nondescript small towns for a burger. From the greasy table where we sat waiting for the food to be dumped in front of us by the over-plump waitress, I stared out of the window.

Opposite was a scruffy house, roof tiles peeling, cladding falling off, windows cracked. But it was home to a large, swarthy-looking family. The kids, half a dozen of them, were playing in the yard. A man was tinkering with the engine of an ancient rusty automobile. The bonnet was raised; the doors were open and the radio was blaring. A large lady, presumably Momma, bustled in and out, alternately yelling at the kids, then at the man with his head in the engine. Who were they? Why did they live there? What did their lives add up to? Did they believe in God? Probably not. Doubtless they lived their lives never having wrestled with the questions that had recently torn my heart apart. Faith to them was as irrelevant as the family with the motor home sitting in the greasy spoon opposite. God might or might not exist for them, and who cares? Right and wrong would be purely a matter of pragmatics, certainly not divinely prescribed absolutes. How many different men had sired those children? Was the mechanic married to Big Momma? Would it make a fig of difference if he was not?

The words of my morning reading from Job had perhaps prompted my thoughts:

Why do the wicked live on? Their homes are safe and free from fear. They see their children established around them. They sing to the music of tambourine and harp, their little ones dance about. They spend their years in prosperity and go down to the grave in peace. Yet they say to God, 'Leave us alone! We have no desire to know your ways. Who is the Almighty, that we should serve him? What would we gain by praying to him?'

The burgers arrived, and my morbid thoughts were quenched by a cola-induced sugar rush. Appetites assuaged, we stepped out to return to the motor home by the kerbside. We were buffeted by a gust of wind which blew dust into our eyes. A clump of tumbleweed rolled down the middle of the road, and loose straw swirled about. The bonnet of the car in the house opposite banged shut and the man shouted at the children, who scurried away round the back of the house. *'Yet how often is the lamp of the wicked snuffed out? How often does calamity come upon them? How often are they like straw before the wind, like chaff swept away by a gale?'*

God no more calls them to account than do I! Is God just? Then why does he not insist on justice?

We drove on for what seemed like days. 'Are we still in America?' Dan would ask. You can drive across England in an afternoon. We had never seen so much of nothing. I had lived most of my life in the south of England, a small world full of self-importance. The sheer size of North America was beginning to cause my question-mark to shrink. If the world was so much bigger than I had previously experienced, then perhaps my questions were less important than

I had thought. '*Have you comprehended the vast expanses of the earth? Can you probe the limits of the Almighty? They are higher than the heavens . . . deeper than the depths . . . longer than the earth and wider than the sea.*'

God did more for Job by showing him the scale of his creation than he did by arguing theology! He was perhaps doing the same for me.

'Who dug the Grand Canyon, Dad?' asked Becky, when eventually we arrived and stood on its lip.

'Fred.'

'Why?'

'Well, Fred was a Scotsman, and one day he dropped a penny . . .' I could always become a tour guide if I never made it back to preaching!

We made camp by a dry stream bed in a small canyon in the desert. We were fascinated by the crumbling cliffs and dramatic rock formations that millennia of erosion had carved. As the afternoon faded to night we lit a fire and sat by it on an old fallen tree, toasting marshmallows, singing 'Home on the Range', then just watching the firelight flickering on the rocks. Esther was restless, lighting the end of her stick and whirring it around, making patterns in the darkness with the glowing tip.

'Since you are so full of energy, Esther, chuck another log on the fire.' A shower of sparks caused Becky to start back from the blaze.

'*Man is born to trouble as surely as sparks fly upward!*' I wonder if Job ever toasted marshmallows with his three friends? Doubtless, trouble had killed the joy of such simple pleasures. '*Man is of few days and full of trouble.*' Yes, life is hard and then you die. As it was for Job, so it still is. Quintin Carr, Jack Stordy, Walter Moss. Life was hard and then they died, just like the old tree we were sitting on. '*At least there is hope for a tree: If it is cut down, it will sprout again. If a man dies, will he live again?*'

Job was still leading my thoughts. Throughout the first thirty-eight dismal chapters there were pinpricks of hope, sparks of positive faith.

'*All the days of my hard service I will wait for my renewal to come.*'

Though my trust in God was at a low ebb, there were still flashes of hope which stabbed the night like sparks, patterns like Esther's glowing stick. But the darkness was pervasive. My confidence had been eroded, my faith had crumbled, my hopes had washed away, and presumably God was responsible. Even Job agreed: '*As a mountain erodes and crumbles and as a rock is moved from its place, as water wears away stones and torrents wash away the soil, so you destroy man's hope.*'

Evening has its own brand of melancholy. Dawn brings hope.

I woke early next day and crept out for a walk before the children were awake. The stars were still visible, but the eastern horizon was brightening. I scrambled up a steep slope in the half-light and then headed along a cliff top. It was cold so I walked briskly. After half an hour I pulled up sharp on the very edge of the world. The Grand Canyon yawned at my feet, all filled with purple shadows and mystery. Terrifying cliffs dropped away to the bottom of creation. I sat down on a rock and watched the sun come up over the horizon, spilling its brilliance into the gloom. I pulled out my pocket Bible and read Job. '*Where were you when I laid the earth's foundation? Tell me, if you under-stand. Who marked off its dimensions? Surely you know!*

Who stretched a measuring line across it? On what were its footings set, or who laid its cornerstone while the morning stars sang together and all the angels shouted for joy?'

God was not limited by my understanding. What if neither I nor the world's greatest minds had much idea of how the world came to be? Did that diminish the wonder of it? Did God owe me an explanation of how or even why he had made it? Of course not! So why should my analytical mind reject a Creator who declined to explain his methods? Wonder and gratitude welled up in me, dispelling logic. What do you do with gratitude if there is no one to thank? 'I'm an atheist, thank God!' has a hollow ring. My, but if there were no God it would be necessary to invent one, just to give expression to worship.

Worship! Such a primitive instinct. But then, so is hunger or fatigue, and the desire for food and sleep is as much a vital part of life for sophisticated twentieth-century dwellers as it was for cavemen. And those instincts correspond to the objective realities which our bodies need for survival. Why, therefore, should the ancient instinct to worship not correspond to an objective reality? Why should God alone be suspected of being less than an objective reality demanded by a universal instinct? Or perhaps in this day of enlightenment we should also rise above the needs for food and sleep, writing them off as 'primitive'!

A movement below caught my eye. I stood up and looked over the edge. A huge bird was flying a few hundred feet below where I stood. Fancy that! Being able to look down at the eagles!

'Does the eagle soar at your command and build his nest on high? He dwells on a cliff and stays there at night; a rocky crag is his stronghold. From there he seeks

out his food; his eyes detect it from afar.'

A primitive instinct began to poke its head through my wonder. It must be breakfast-time.

When I got back, Dan was still sleeping on the kitchen table and no amount of prodding and tickling would cause him to stir. I needed that space for my cornflakes. So I scooped him up, still in his sleeping bag, carried him outside and shook him out into a snow bank. *'Have you ever given orders to the morning that it might take the earth by the edges and shake the wicked out of it?'*

'Incongruous' is the only word that seems to fit. London Bridge in the desert! The children wanted to know who moved it there, and who was there to blame but Fred?

My question was less 'Who?' and more 'Why?' Why would anyone want to move an obsolete bridge, with a historic reputation for structural weakness, from spanning the Thames to spanning nothing but sand? Had they used their amazing American ingenuity to stretch it sufficiently to span the Grand Canyon, then perhaps there might be room for understanding. But from nowhere to nowhere? Made no sense.

Our curiosity was satisfied after a brief inspection. Apparently it was all a costly mistake for a millionaire who had imagined himself to be buying Tower Bridge. My, but he must have been disappointed when he put all the pieces together and there was just an ordinary old bridge, no towers, no nothing! But Joy and I needed to stretch our legs after long confinement in the motor home, so we abandoned Esther, Dan and Becky in a play area and sauntered off for a stroll.

'I suppose there is no more answer to the question of

why this bridge is here than there is to the question of why God made the world. Clearly somebody made it. It didn't just happen, pouf! and there it was, any more than London Bridge is a freak product of the evolution of the Arizona landscape. But did God make the world just to satisfy some divine whim of fancy, or does it have purpose?'

I recalled that ancient road I had followed to Greshornish Point a few months back, how I had at first imagined it to be no more than a sheep track, but eventually realised that it had purpose and that it led somewhere.

'Future archaeologists might one day be led to believe that once a great river flowed through here, and with this bridge for evidence it wouldn't be difficult to argue. But they would be wrong. Were we wrong to conclude that God had purpose when he made the world? Doesn't the Bible itself suggest that life is meaningless? *"Enjoy life with your wife, whom you love, all the days of this meaningless life that God has given you under the sun – all your meaningless days. For this is your lot in life and in your toilsome labour under the sun. 'Meaningless! Meaningless!' says the Teacher. 'Utterly meaningless! Everything is meaningless.'"* '

'Now don't you ruin a good stroll by getting all cynical again. I thought the clouds were beginning to lift.'

'Well, things are improving,' I admitted. 'I am amazed that God never answered any of Job's questions. Thirty-something chapters of misery and uncertainty, and the book ends with no answers given.'

'There were no answers given to the questions "Why?" or "How?", but the last few chapters are big on answering "Who?" And it seems that was enough for Job. He was satisfied and asked no more questions, raised no more cynical objections, ruined no more walks with his wife.'

'Do you think I have been asking the wrong questions then?'

'Frankly, yes. You have been so intent on asking "Why this?" and "Why that?", "Why did God let Max break his neck?" and "Why didn't he heal him?" You have put God on trial and demanded that he justify his actions to you. And consequently, your estimation of God has shrunk. You put yourself on the judgment throne and God in the dock, an inflated idea of your own significance and a terribly withered idea of God's.'

What can you say in the face of such wisdom? After a few minutes of silent wandering and pondering, my mouth clicked into gear: 'But there are some things that we have to talk about some time, like what we are going to do when we get home. We can't be nomads for the rest of our lives. How are we going to earn a living? I doubt I will be able to preach again.'

'You could go back to your original career, into commercial flying.'

'Yes, that's a possibility.' I stopped for a moment and looked Joy in the face. 'Do you think God minds what we do? I mean, if he's so great and declines to answer our petty questions about how and why, do we need to place such emphasis on those same questions ourselves? "How are we going to make a living?" Do you think he cares if we preach the gospel or fly aeroplanes? "*Can a man be of benefit to God? What pleasure would it give the Almighty if you were righteous? Is not God in the heights of heaven? What does God know? Does he judge through such darkness? He does not see us as he goes about in the vaulted heavens.*" It seems God is just too big to be bothered with petty questions of what we do with our lives. Perhaps he just gives us the freedom to get on with it as best we can.'

'So let's just make our own choices.'

'Without any reference to God, for his divine guidance?'

Joy was silent. We had both been raised to believe that God's will should always be sought when making important decisions.

'You're not comfortable with that, are you, Joy? I can see you're not. Well the truth is, neither am I. If God, who I concede might be there, isn't interested in what to us are huge decisions, then why does the Bible say he keeps an inventory of the hairs on our heads?' Joy was still silent. 'If everything we do is merely up to us and God is neither pleased nor disappointed, then all the great missionaries who have sacrificed their lives, responding to a missionary call to some far-flung corner of the globe – well, they might as well have stayed home for all that God cares. There is no such thing as a divine commission, no call for passionate self-sacrifice in God's service. Let's just make a living in the most convenient way we can find and leave saving the world to a few mistaken religious fanatics.'

'But there is more to it than that, isn't there, Jay?' Joy said quietly.

'I want to believe there is.'

'It's coming, Jay. It's coming.'

After a few more silent minutes: 'But how are we to know what God's will is? The Bible says we are to honour our parents, but it was my mother's wishful thinking, taking verses out of context, that has been in part responsible for throwing me into a loop. She used those words to act as a kind of prophecy that I would preach the gospel, and so deeply is that still burned into my soul that to do anything other is like a denial of my destiny. Yet when I think about it rationally I see that the reason for believing myself as commissioned by God to preach the gospel is questionable at best, taken out of context and an abuse of the Bible.'

'Jay, supposing you were to receive a command to preach the gospel other than via your mother's Bible reading?'

'What do you mean? An echoey voice from the sky?'

'No. I was just thinking that Jesus said, with all authority: "Go, preach the gospel!" If he said that with all authority, then somehow that would eclipse, or, better yet, embrace your mother's "commission" in his "Great Commission". There would be no conflict of interest, for you could abandon your mother's out-of-context promise in favour of Jesus' universal command and still continue in the same direction.'

'Go, preach the gospel . . .' Simple obedience seemed much more attractive than living in frustrated expectation that a miracle would one day happen to transform bumbling, tongue-tied me into Billy Graham. Yes. I could live with that. I would return to preach the gospel, not because Mother promised me a miracle, but simply out of obedience to what was written.

And then the two-by-four hit me again. How could I preach a gospel, calling others to believe in someone whose existence I myself doubted?

Driving through a small town next day we noticed a store calling itself 'Rockhound's Paradise'. Outside, there was a model of an old prospector panning for gold.

'We have to stop!' Joy insisted. We came out half an hour later armed with a map, a book on precious stones and a pointy hammer – essential equipment for prospectors like ourselves. We followed a trackway out into the desert, eventually settling for a spot not dissimilar to every other spot we could see for fifty miles in any direction. There was nothing and nobody to be seen or heard. We explored our environment, leery of rattlesnakes, reassured by the thought that they sleep in the cold, yet terrified lest we should wake one up. If Daniel's waking moments were anything to go by, then a snake might not be too friendly either if disturbed.

We didn't find gold, but we did pick up some beautiful rocks shot through with swirls of red and orange. They still remain by our fireplace to this day, more precious than gold, for they recall a happy family day, working together as prospectors in a foreign land.

When evening came and the children were tightly wedged into their bunks or neatly laid on their table, Joy and I took a stroll in the gathering darkness. An extra-ordinary feeling of being completely alone engulfed us. There was no light to remind us of the rest of the human race; no noise of passing vehicles, for there were none; not a breath of wind. Just absolute stillness. Above us was the vastness of space. We felt dwarfed and insignificant.

Who was I to question the Creator? He might question my right to existence, but how arrogant of me to query his.

Can you bind the beautiful Pleiades? Can you loose the cords of Orion? Can you bring forth the constellations in their seasons or lead out the Bear with its cubs? Do you know the laws of the heavens? Can you set up God's dominion over the earth? He spreads out the northern skies over empty space; he suspends the earth over nothing. He marks out the horizon for a boundary

between light and darkness. And these are but the outer
fringe of his works!

A God capable of creating infinite space! If my mind was
incapable of conceiving what logic told me was right there
before my eyes – infinity – then how could I ever hope to
get my brain round the Creator of infinity! One can only
walk so far in the shoes of reason till eventually one is
forced to turn back or continue barefoot on the holy ground
of faith.

If the infinity above our heads was but the outer fringes
of his work, then how would it be to see him face to face?

Suddenly, at the same moment, Joy and I were both
gripped in unimaginable terror. We turned and fled back to
the motor home, slammed the door behind us, turned on all
the lights and cranked the radio. I don't think it was so
much a supernatural experience as a wholly natural one.
We city dwellers live surrounded by noise and people.
Rarely are we completely alone, facing the great, lonely,
forgotten places. Our sky is the ceiling above our heads,
our horizon the TV screen. Little wonder God gets crowded
out.

Before we went to sleep I had a brief consultation with
Job.

'*Then the* LORD *spoke to Job: "Brace yourself like a
man; I will question you, and you shall answer me. Would
you discredit my justice? Would you condemn me to justify
yourself?"* '

That was exactly what I had done. I had sought to
discredit God in order to justify myself. 'If there is no God
after all, then I need trust him no longer. If, on the other
hand, there is a God, then either he doesn't keep his

promises or there is something wrong with me. Therefore, God must be a promise-breaker, for there's nothing wrong with me!' How arrogant I was.

Then Job replied to the LORD: 'I know that you can do all things; no plan of yours can be thwarted. You asked, "Who is this that obscures my counsel without knowledge?" Surely I spoke of things I did not understand, things too wonderful for me to know. You said, "Listen now, and I will speak; I will question you, and you shall answer me." My ears had heard of you but now my eyes have seen you. Therefore I despise myself and repent in dust and ashes.'

'God,' I whispered, 'If you hear me, I'm so sorry.' The stars looked down from infinity through the window of our tiny home, and the surrounding desert was silent.

Next day it was over the mountains and down to the sparkling waters of the Pacific. No more snow or desert – palm trees and green grass, flowers and songbirds.

We headed straight for the beach. As we stood on the glistening sand in our bare feet, we looked in awe at the huge waves which were rolling in from the Pacific, all the way from China. As families have done since time was young, we would follow out a receding wave, then flee back up the beach as another threatened to swamp us. The ground shook as the waves broke and the wind whipped the spume into our faces. Becky hung back with Joy. Her legs were shorter than those of her older brother and sister. 'What's the matter, Beck?' Dan taunted. 'You're not scared, are you?'

'The waves are so big they might come and wash us all away,' she said, clinging to Joy's skirt.

'Don't worry, Beck,' Joy reassured her. 'The waves won't reach us.'

'*Who shut up the sea behind doors when I fixed limits for it, when I said, "This far you may come and no farther; here is where your proud waves halt"?*' Would Job never mind his own business?

Peter Letchford's friend in San Diego made us welcome. He arranged for us to park the motor home in the car park of his church. We could not believe our British eyes when we saw the size of it. It was bigger than two soccer pitches. 'What a ridiculous waste of space.' But when Sunday came and it was full by 8.30 in the morning, before we were even up, we changed our minds. At the close of the first service it emptied out, only to be refilled by a new set of cars. We had never dreamed that so many people would come together to worship. 'And this is by no means the biggest church in town,' our host told us.

We could hardly not attend. First there was Sunday School. We got the children settled and then followed directions to an adult class.

There were a couple of hundred people comfortably seated in theatre-style seats in a mini amphitheatre. It was as comfortable a place as any to kill an hour doing our duty. Notices and a few laughs, and the teacher was introduced: a local psychiatrist who would be talking about bitterness, depression and doubt. Now there was a relevant theme. If this was like my last brush with a psychiatrist, he would soon be diagnosing chemical imbalance and pre-scribing a three-month holiday and some little yellow pills.

I was pleasantly surprised, therefore, when he opened his Bible and showed us with clear logic that there was a definite and unmistakable link between bitterness and depression, and between depression and doubt. It starts with a conflict between people. Anger, if repressed and bottled up, becomes bitterness. Bitterness, if allowed to fester, becomes depression. Depression leads to all sorts of things, including doubting and loss of faith in God.

The solution he recommended was not medical, but rather to forgive. 'Go to the cause of the doubt and the depression. Don't simply address the symptoms. And don't procrastinate. If you have something against someone, then the longer you leave it unresolved the more it will fester. Take responsibility and do something about it this very day!'

Coffee was served out in the foyer. 'But Dr Foulks told me that my doubts were the result of a chemical imbalance in the brain,' I hissed at Joy as we tried to prevent the jostling throng jogging our arms and spilling our coffee on the lush pink carpet.

The best of chemical imbalances is that you can blame on them what you like. My body chemistry was to blame for my unbelief in God. I was not responsible! On the other hand, the worst of what we had heard that morning was that I *was* responsible, and could therefore blame no one else, not even my own internal chemicals.

'From what that man was saying, both could be true. Remember how he said that anger and bitterness release certain harmful chemicals into the system which can do physical damage as well as emotional? Maybe that's what has happened to us.' Joy always identified herself as thinking like me, never as one step superior. It was as if she felt the doubts as keenly as I. So it was always 'us' rather than 'you'. I guess that is how Jesus helped us from our sin to his righteousness. He identified with sinners. I am blessed to have a wife 'who could be touched with the feeling of my infirmity'.

'That would mean that unresolved conflicts could be the cause of our troubles,' I agreed. 'But I can't think of anyone I feel angry with, can you? All this is good theory, but I can't see how it fits in with our situation.'

'Perhaps we ought to pray and ask God to bring to our minds anyone we may be bitter against.'

Joy did the praying as we sat in the sanctuary in hushed anticipation of the service. My mind didn't click into the worship, for I was bombarded for the next hour by a constant mental procession of people I was still angry with. I was amazed to find that I had been angry with the Hildenborough Council of Management for not lifting the burden of the place from me sooner. I was angry with Felicity Lane for always being right. I was angry with my friends for having failed to understand my doubts and having been unable to give me solutions to them. I was angry with Christians in general for their naive expectations and their gullible acceptance of any crackpot theory to hit the Christian scene. Most of all, I was angry with God himself for having let me down repeatedly. He had allowed three men I had loved and admired to die. He had broken Max's neck and then raised my expectation of a miraculous healing, only to disappoint me. He had made a fool of me over the finances of the Hildenborough expansion programme. He had put false expectations before me over Broughton Manor. The words of Jeremiah came to mind: *'O Lord, you have deceived me and I was deceived. You are stronger than I, and you have prevailed. I have become a laughingstock all the day; everyone mocks me.'*

It dawned on me afresh just how ridiculous it was for me to be angry with God. A good portion of my unbelief in God had been a way of hitting out at him. 'You don't play fair, God, so I'm not playing any more. If you won't do what I want then I refuse to believe in you, so there!' I hadn't harmed him at all but had done terrible damage to myself and those I loved.

I pulled out the Bible from the rack screwed to the back of the pew in front. And there was Job, just before the Psalms, right where he always was. Perhaps psalms of praise might follow my troubles also: '*Look up at the heavens and see; If you sin, how does that affect him? If your sins are many, what does that do to him? Your wickedness affects only a man like yourself.'*

Forgiveness was the prescription, so at the close of the service I asked God to forgive me my trespasses as I forgave those who had trespassed against me.

During the afternoon we visited Seaworld. The walrus spat seawater all over Daniel. Dolphins jumped through hoops. The killer whale kissed the trainer. '*Can you pull in the leviathan with a fishhook? Can you make a pet of him like a bird or put him on a leash for your girls? Any hope of subduing him is false. Who then is able to stand against me?*'

Well, the killer whale's fat kiss on the trainer's cheek blew a hole in that argument! But I suppose Job never visited Seaworld!

That night the church car park filled up again. Our host called in and offered to arrange baby-sitters so we could attend the service. We accepted, and Esther, Dan and Becky jumped happily into the back seat of a huge station wagon.

I got more into the evening service. It was less formal. The pastor was teaching about worry. 'Insistence on our own rights is the chief cause of worry,' he said. Insistence on my rights hadn't done my peace of mind any good. Hadn't I seen it as my right to expect God to answer my prayer for the staff and the money needed at Hildenborough? Wasn't it invariably a sense of threatened rights which had made me clash with Felicity? Hadn't I seen Broughton Manor as a right to be demanded because I thought God had promised it?

The pastor defined worry as the taking of responsibilities which God never intended us to carry. Freedom from worry comes from the surrender of all our rights and all our loved ones to God. If he owns our rights, then we have no further need to worry. If he takes the responsibility for our loved ones, then we need not stagger under a responsibility only God is strong enough to bear.

Suddenly a notice flashed up on the screen behind the pastor: 'Would Justyn Rees please contact the San Diego General Hospital immediately.'

We could think of only three reasons for such a summons – Esther, Daniel or Rebecca. We pushed our way conspicuously out of our pew and hurried and worried and carried responsibilities which God never intended us to carry. How would we arrange the funeral? Would we fly the body home or bury it here?

In the emergency waiting-room we found Daniel with a slight cut on his finger, self-inflicted while peeling an orange! The nurse required a parent's signature before applying a Band-Aid.

Eventually we laughed and conceded the point. Rights were best given to God to be carried by him.

Next morning I awoke to a realisation that something was changing. The sky was bluer and the oranges on the tree outside the motor home were oranger. Perhaps life was worth the living after all. We were making progress.

With the success of Seaworld still fresh in our minds, we headed for the San Diego zoo, which turned out to be undoubtedly the best zoo we had ever seen.

'Who cleans out all these animals?' asked Esther, eyes round with wonder as she drew mental comparison with the weekly mess in her rabbit hutch.

'Fred.'

The leopard paced endlessly up and down. The lions slept in the sun. The snakes – well, they might as well have been plastic for all the action we observed. The chimps swung and the camel munched. The rhino scratched his backside against a concrete rock and the elephants towered over all, sauntering majestically around their enclosure.

Do you know when the mountain goats give birth? Do you watch when the doe bears her fawn? Do you give the horse his strength or clothe his neck with a flowing mane? Look at the behemoth, which I made along with you. What strength he has in his loins, what power in the muscles of his belly! His tail sways like a ceda. His bones are tubes of bronze, his limbs like rods of iron. He ranks first among the works of God.

San Diego proved to be a great place to be tourists, so we hung around for a week. We could park in the church car park for free, so we were in no hurry to move on. Wednesday evening offered a midweek meeting. Child-care facilities were on offer, so we went.

The same pastor who had taught on Sunday night was speaking. 'Death of a vision' was his theme. Abraham had received a God-given vision of innumerable descendants. He had done his human uttermost to father even one child and had failed. *Death of a vision!* Then God gave them Isaac. Joseph had a vision of greatness but found himself first a slave, then a convict in an Egyptian jail. *Death of a vision!* Next day God made him prime minister. Moses had visualised himself as liberator of Israel from Egyptian slavery. He failed so miserably in his human attempt that he had to live the next forty years in the backside of the desert as a fugitive from a murder rap. *Death of a vision!* Then one day when he was a senior citizen he noticed a bush on fire which wouldn't burn . . .

'Much of the strategy of Satan is to get us to seek to do God's work in our own strength,' the pastor told us. 'But God never allows us to bring about his solutions by human effort or ingenuity. Gideon had to send 31,700 volunteers home, leaving only a bare 300 to fight the Midianites lest human pride could have had opportunity to vaunt itself.'

Out in the car park later that evening I lay on my bed gazing at the ceiling, contemplating my vision. It was not difficult to identify. I had always sensed the call to preach the gospel ever since my mother had read me those verses from Luke 1. I, too, had done my very best to fulfil the vision, and had worked myself into the floor in the attempt. My best efforts, and Hildenborough was closed down. *Death of a vision!* Would God work a miracle and do it his way?

* * *

As we drove north from San Diego we were conscious that a change had taken place. My faith was growing – or rather, the doubts were shrinking. What had brought this about? It was hard to put a finger on it. I had imagined that the cure, if there were to be one, would be sudden spiritual revelation. Faith, being a gift of God, would doubtless descend upon me like a dove. But it was not turning out like that. It was just that doubt was receding like an ebbing tide. The all-pervasive question-mark was smaller. It was not questions being answered that was shrinking the swelling, but rather that other things, natural things, true things, beautiful things, were growing, crowding out the negative, the hurt, the anger. That had been God's therapy for Job, a nature walk with the Creator! And now he was doing it for me.

And, yes! the teaching at the San Diego church didn't do us any harm either. A good dose of practical common sense. There were no wild claims of divine revelation, no exaggerated coincidences to swallow, no display of dubious miracles to try to see through or to attempt to muster sufficient faith to believe. Each of the presentations had been reasonable, wise judgment and common sense. That was the kind of faith I could respect and actually wished to make my own. It was the kind of faith which would result in responsible, godly living.

You cannot visit California without a trip to Disneyland. We made our pilgrimage thither. 'Fantastic' is the most appropriate description, for it is fantasy at its very best. Everything is smaller than life except Mickey Mouse, who turned out to be considerably larger than Daniel had imagined. There is a miniature Matterhorn, containing a hair-raising train ride which could make even a Swiss engineer blanch. There is the New Orleans river boat, the Small World and the Mad Hatter's Tea Party.

The children loved it, but I was in the wrong frame of mind. Its falsehood disturbed me. In other circumstances I would have been as much a kid as any of them, but I was just in the process of escaping from a make-believe faith which had nearly destroyed my relationship with God. It had been a Disneyland version of the New Testament which had so turned me off, the land of spiritual make-believe where you must believe even that which is obviously not true, the land of 'fake it till you make it'.

What I wanted was real mountains rather than concrete Matterhorns and plastic snow. So we headed further north to Yosemite National Park and arrived to find the main campsite under three feet of real snow. The place was deserted, which in the circumstances was hardly surprising. Cold reality often discourages the crowds. It discouraged us, too, so we drove to the other campsite to find it deserted by both snow and fellow campers. The whole park was ours and we had it to ourselves. We decided to put down roots. Staying in one place for over a week was roots for the nomadic Rees family.

There was everything we could want: a river to paddle in if we could stand the cold, rocks to climb, melting snow banks to slide down, endless trails to explore, even bears to imagine prowling around at night, though we never actually saw one. But we did see 'Smoky the bear', a real park ranger in pursuit of thieves who had apparently shared our campsite for one night of our stay. They had stolen a motor home just like ours and had invaded the privacy of our several-thousand-acre campsite. We were all terribly excited and gave vivid descriptions of the people we had seen, then locked our door tight at night for fear they might come back.

It was in the majestic beauty of this setting that a great peace began to steal into my soul. Even though I had been faithless, God had remained faithful. Prayer began to be less a soliloquy and more a genuine communication with God.

One morning, while the children were paddling happily in a stream, Joy and I sat on a rock in the sunshine and prayed. We prayed together and out loud. That must have been a first for over a year. We prayed about this and that, and then started to concentrate on the children. This was natural enough, for they were playing in the centre of our field of vision. Esther was nine, and had asked the Lord Jesus to come into her heart and make her a Christian a year or so previously. She had been talking to her cousin Sarah at the time. Though she was a young child, the experience had been very real to her. But Daniel, who was seven, and Becky, who was just five, had never shown any initiative in that direction thus far. How very concerned I had been through those terrible months for their future spiritual development. Would my doubting ruin their chances of following the Lord themselves? But that day, sitting on the rock, we both prayed that my lapse would in no way affect their walk with the Lord adversely and that in due time he would bring Daniel and Becky to receive Jesus into their lives just as Esther had already done.

That afternoon we went for a walk downriver. Daniel had discovered that empty pop cans carried a ransom on their heads, a reclaimable deposit. A whole winter's worth of discarded cans was just being revealed by the melting snow. So with all the zeal of the old-time California gold prospectors, we set off. Esther was not nearly so mercenary, but Dan and Becky ran this way and that till they had nearly filled a plastic garbage sack each. Exhausted and satisfied with our 'strike', we turned for home.

'Mum,' said Dan, 'when did you become a Christian?' She told him.

'Could I ask Jesus into my heart?'

I was walking ahead with Esther so I missed this conversation. The first I knew of it was when Dan came running to catch me up to tell me that he had just asked Jesus to come into his heart. Hot on his heels was Becky, who, not to be outdone by her big brother, had followed suit.

Was it just coincidence that we prayed as we had that very morning? Was it some form of thought transference? Or could it be that God had laid that prayer on our hearts, and had answered it so clearly that even a doubting cynic like me could not fail to see the coincidence?

Delightful days which blend into a hazy memory of family happiness passed, till the nomadic instinct got the better of us once again and we moved on. Over the mountains we went, heading east this time. After five days of travel we took a day off. It being Sunday morning we sought out a church, then headed for the nearest state park. That parks were a success we were all agreed. The map suggested that this one was good for fishing, but expectations were not met. It turned out to be little more than a muddy pond, and the whole place had that rundown, overgrown look of neglect. Nevertheless, we were determined to cook our Sunday lunch and make the very best of a bad job. We set off to drive down a little track which ran along a hillside sloping down to the water's edge on one side of the lake. It wasn't till the wheels started to spin that we realised just how muddy the track was. I slipped into reverse, hoping to back out of trouble, but the only motion I achieved was sideways. Back and forth I shunted, till we slid right off the track and the whole motor home tilted at an alarming angle.

'Everyone out!' I shouted. The lack of Sunday lunch rendered me bad tempered. The impossibility of cooking it on a stove which inclined like the side of a house rendered Joy bad tempered. Wading through the mud from the motor home's door delighted the children. It was that red, sticky, slimy mud which clumps up on the soles of trainers till they resemble moon boots.

So what were we to do? We couldn't move. We couldn't cook. We couldn't lie down and have a rest. The children couldn't come and go freely because of the mud. We were stuck in every way imaginable. There was no nearby town from which we could hope to get help, and anyway, it was Sunday, so most places would be shut.

'Why don't we pray about it?' suggested Esther piously. My first angry instinct was to tell her that if she couldn't think of anything sensible to say, then she should shut up. Mercifully I refrained, and with Joy leading the way we did pray, a very practical and very specific prayer, just the kind of prayer I had avoided for months.

'O Lord, we're stuck. Please help us to get out of here without damaging the motor home.'

Scarcely had we said 'amen' when there was a hoot and a 'hello'.

'Hey! Are you folks stuck?'

'Sure are,' we replied, agreeing the obvious.

There was a red-faced man in a Jeep, on the front of which was a powerful winch. Within five minutes we were on solid ground.

'Mum,' whispered Becky, tugging at Joy's skirt, 'we were just praying about that.'

The whole family crowded round the red-faced man to express our gratitude.

'I'm Justyn Rees, and we are all from England. What's your name?'

The children's jaws dropped and there was a moment of awed silence when he replied simply: 'Fred.' So we had finally met him!

'Is he an angel?' whispered Becky, still clinging to Joy's dress.

So it seemed that coincidences abounded – or perhaps God was interested in the practical things of life after all.

Our safari eventually came to an end. We shipped the motor home to England and boarded a jet ourselves. When the motor home caught us up, we sold it for twice the price we had originally paid when it was brand new. The profit covered the cost of shipping, import duty, all our air fares out and back, plus a total cost of fuel, food and extras for the whole three months of our adventure. The entire trip had cost us not one brass farthing. There was even a small surplus left over.

So God did care about us and was concerned even for matters of finance. None of these coincidences proved anything to us, for had we experienced them while I was still in a state of unbelief, I doubt we should have even noticed them. But coming as they did so soon after my faith had begun to revive, they acted as confirmations of what I was already believing. How very kind God is.

12

Preach Faith Till You Have It!

After three months away it was quite an adjustment to be back in England. For one thing, home was different. Just before leaving for the US we had sold Munda, which had been so conveniently situated right next to the Hildenborough Hall property. We therefore needed to find a new house to call home. Our search ended at the Old Vicarage, a 500-year-old ruin in the picturesque village of Shoreham. Hildenborough was also different. I was no longer General Director and a new manager had been appointed by the Council of Management to be responsible for operations. He was occupying my old office and I was in the way. It was an odd feeling.

Max was in great form. The three months had done him a power of good. He was stronger and had a new sense of calling to the ministry of evangelism. He had written a book called *Halfway to Heaven* (Hodder & Stoughton, 1982), recording and exploring the experience of breaking his neck. Consequently, he was in great demand to speak at dinner parties and events of all kinds. He no longer needed me to carry his bags, for he had learned to drive himself. His Ford Granada had been specially modified to favour his stronger left leg, with the accelerator and the brake pedals reversed – an adaptation which caused car thieves considerable embarrassment when they attempted to make off with it.

My dilemma was that I seemed to be redundant. Where did I fit? Who would ever invite me to preach? And if they did, would I have anything to say?

So I withdrew to the Old Vicarage to get the packing cases unpacked and order restored. The kitchen was chaos and Joy didn't feel like cooking, so we went over the road to the George and Dragon for a pub lunch.

'So you are the new owners of the Old Vicarage, are you,' said Lionel, the landlord. 'I hope you like it.'

'You sound a little dubious about that,' I returned.

'Oh, not dubious exactly. No. It's just that none of the previous owners have stayed there for very long.'

'I suppose you're going to tell us it's haunted or something.'

'I don't hold with that sort of nonsense. But . . .'

'But what?'

'Something strange happens to the electrical appliances from time to time.'

'Sounds like a rewire might help more than an exorcism.'

Some friends from New Zealand came to stay with us. They were our first house guests and we proudly showed them into the guest room, which was in the wing of the house nearest to the George and Dragon. They came down to breakfast next morning white and shaken.

'So, how did you sleep?'

'Is this house haunted, by any chance?' they stammered.

'Only by the landlord of the George.'

'No, seriously. Has anything unusual happened here before?'

'What do you mean by "unusual"?'

'Well, in the middle of the night we heard the radio blaring in the kitchen. So I went down to investigate, to find all the lights on and no one to be seen. All the doors and windows were locked, so no one could have got in.'

'So what did you do?'

'Well, we turned them all off and went back to bed, thinking that some kind of timer must have triggered it. We were just dozing off when my electric razor was turned on at the other side of the room. Of course, we snapped on the light, but there was no one there. We haven't slept a wink since.'

We never got to the bottom of the mystery.

The five hundred years of history of the house was hard to trace, but we unearthed a few fascinating facts. Two hundred years previously, John Wesley, the great Methodist preacher, had stayed there on a number of occasions. He had preached outside the George and Dragon to the crowds, who had not appreciated his message and had thrown him in the river. Electricity not having been invented at that time, we doubted if there was a connection between Wesley's wetting and the phantom electrician.

The Reverend Perronet, the vicar of Shoreham during the mid-1700s, had introduced Wesley to the lady who later became his wife – a singularly unhappy marriage, so not a glorious chapter in the house's history.

Most intriguing was the discovery that in our dining room John Wesley had established a flourishing Bible class, a gathering to which new believers could come together to study and pray. If there were ghosts from the past, then I was far more interested in the memories of Wesley than in a jinx in the wiring. If the Holy Ghost could change a whole nation through the preaching of this one man, then that was worthy of note.

Inspired by the Wesley connection, I purchased a copy of John Wesley's journal. Sitting in the very room where, a couple of centuries previously, he may well have made some of the original entries, I was fascinated to read that he too had struggled with faith in God. His determination to shake the doubts had led him to go as a missionary to America. It seemed that America could be regarded as the panacea for all doubters! While there, he had gone through some dark times, wondering about the validity of his mission and tormented over his own relationship with God. He returned to England a disillusioned man.

As was true in my experience, bad news had compounded poor Wesley's doubts. Soon after his return, he had received word that his brother Charles was dying, so had set off post haste to visit him in Oxford. But better news awaited him, for he found Charles on the road to recovery from his pleurisy. Perhaps God did answer prayer, after all.

It was his entries written while he was in Oxford that especially caught my interest. It may have been frustration with his failed career as a missionary, or it may have been shock at his near bereavement, but he found himself profoundly depressed. There was the man who would soon become England's greatest evangelist, in much the same slough as I had been. What was he to do? What kind of profession could a failed missionary pursue? That was precisely my dilemma. What could I, a failed evangelist, do?

His own words describe his turmoil: 'Immediately it struck into my mind, "Leave off preaching. How can you preach to others, who have not faith yourself?"'

God seems to send real flesh-and-blood people to give

reassurance to his children. Peter Böhler was in Oxford, himself a missionary preacher. Wesley wrote: 'I asked Böhler whether he thought I should leave it [preaching] off or not. He answered, "By no means." I asked, "But what can I preach?" He said, "Preach faith till you have it; and then, because you have it, you will preach faith." '

Could a doubter preach faith? Sitting there in our dining room, where Wesley had sat and preached faith to the citizens of Shoreham, I prayed: 'Lord, if you want me to preach again, then please give me an opportunity that I can't ignore.'

Later that morning I was crossing the high street in Sevenoaks when a familiar voice hailed me.

'Hello, Justyn. What are you doing here? I thought you were in America.' It was Peter Larcombe, a local minister.

'Just got back,' I replied, dodging a bus.

'Strange that I should run into you today. Some of our young people were saying to me only yesterday that they would love to be involved in an evangelistic outreach to the area this summer. They were wondering if you might be available to do the preaching' – *an opportunity that I couldn't ignore!*

Mixed emotions were released in my mental cocktail shaker. Elation! Fancy that! The answer to my prayer. Horror! If he knew about my doubts he would never be pursuing this conversation. Standing there, surrounded by busy shoppers, I found myself at a loss for a reply. Eventually I decided that honesty is generally the best policy; confession is good for the soul.

'Peter, do you know where my head has been this past year or so?'

'I've heard rumours, but no, I don't know exactly.'

'I have been in the wilderness. I lost my faith. I quit believing in God.'

'That's what I heard.'

'So, you see, I wouldn't be much good at preaching. I wouldn't know what to say.'

'Justyn, preach faith till you have it; and then, because you have it, you will preach faith.'

'Where did you get that from?' I said, stunned.

'Oh, it's something someone said to John Wesley once.' It seemed Peter Larcombe and Peter Böhler were similarly inspired.

'I'm not sure that I am in a position to call people to a faith in God.'

'Actually, Justyn, it may be that you are better qualified now to speak to unbelievers than you ever were before.'

'How do you figure that?'

'Well, if the Bible is right in saying that he who doubts is like a wave of the sea, buffeted around by the wind, then you know better than most what it feels like to be close to the waves, to struggle between doubts and belief. An evangelist is like a lifeboatman who operates close to the waves so he can reach drowning men. If you are to reach people, you are likely to be more effective if you are near the water than if you tower above them in an unsinkable cruise ship type of faith.'

'You mean my doubts could work for me, rather than against me, as I help doubters to become believers?'

'That is exactly what I mean.'

'Give me time to think it over,' I stalled. 'I'll give you a bell in a day or so.'

Peter hurried off about his business and I went into

Boots the Chemist and headed for the photography section. I had a bulging envelope full of film to be developed so I could bore all our friends with pictures of America. I dumped them all in the desk and received back the little chit from the girl.

'Hello, Justyn!' I swung round and there was Max. 'What are you up to?'

'Nothing special,' I replied. 'How about you? Fancy a walk in the park?'

'I'm with you! Let's take a stroll in Knole Park to boost the appetite, then we could get a bite at the Buck's Head.' The only alternative was more unpacking back at the Old Vicarage, so any excuse was better than none.

It was a beautiful spring morning. The trees were hinting at fresh green and the daffodils bobbed and trumpeted yellow. Max shuffled along with his 'individualistic walking style'.

'So how does it feel to be back?'

'It feels really strange. I don't seem to belong any more. And coming back to Hildenborough brings all the old guilt flooding back. I feel terrible that so many of the staff were put out of work and the whole place has stood empty since last year. And all this just because I wouldn't trust God.'

'But surely it wasn't all your fault, was it?'

'It may not have been my fault, but it was my responsibility to keep the place running and to go on trusting God. Therefore the blame must be mine.'

'But there were good times, weren't there?'

'Well, of course there were good times. You remember how it was before Grandpa died and you broke your neck. There must have been hundreds who came to faith in God during those years.'

'Well then, you are to be congratulated! You must have done a marvellous job!'

'Get real, Max! You know it wasn't me doing a marvellous job, or you for that matter. It was just God doing his thing.'

'Now wait a minute.' Max was puffing a bit, for we had just struggled up a steep incline. He stopped and turned to face me. 'All the good parts were nothing to do with you. It was God alone who did it. Right?'

'OK.'

'But the bad parts were all because you failed in your responsibility. God had nothing to do with them? Is that it?'

'Yes, I suppose that is about the measure of it.'

'Well, if you ask me that seems to be grossly unfair. If God takes the credit when things go right, it's only cricket that he should take the rap when things go wrong. That is what responsibility is all about.'

'What?'

'Did you ever pray about the situation?'

'Why, of course I prayed. You were there praying too, till you broke your silly neck.'

'Then you have no one to blame but God.'

'That sounds rather close to blasphemy, Max!' The words of Elihu, one of Job's friends, seemed to agree with me: *"Far be it from God to do evil ... It is unthinkable that God would do wrong, that the Almighty would pervert justice."* 'How could it possibly be God's fault that Hildenborough was closed down?'

'Maybe not his fault, but certainly his responsibility. If you are not careful you will be in danger of trying to protect God's reputation by taking responsibility for something which only God can carry. It is not necessary to protect God, you know. He can take care of himself.'

'*Will you speak wickedly on God's behalf? Will you speak deceitfully for him? Will you show him partiality? Will you argue the case for God?*'

'But it was sin for me to doubt. I sinned, and that is the root cause of all the trouble.'

'That may be so and the fault therefore is yours, but the responsibility still rests with the one who had the ultimate power to do something about the situation and didn't.'

'Now you really are being blasphemous.'

'No I'm not! Look at it this way: who was to blame for Jesus' crucifixion?'

'Well, Pilate through negligence; the religious leaders because of their unbelief. I suppose we all had a hand in it one way or another.'

'But who was the only one who had power to stop it but didn't?'

'Ultimately God, I suppose.'

'Who was therefore responsible?'

'Do you want me to say that God was responsible?'

'Think about it. Jesus prayed and specifically asked his Father to "let this cup pass from me". Could God have done so?'

'Of course, for God wouldn't be almighty if there was anything he could not do.'

'Then God must have accepted the responsibility for what took place next day. Even in a human court, anyone who knowingly neglects to do everything in his power to avert a disaster is held responsible. How much more so in the supreme court of Heaven.'

'So you mean that while human beings were guilty of the crime of crucifying Jesus, God himself was ultimately responsible, because he could have stopped it, but chose not to.'

'That's exactly it. You might say it was the cost of giving mankind freedom of choice.'

Knole House stood before us, magnificent in the sunshine. The road forked, offering a rough path to the right which would take us around the perimeter wall of the formal gardens, but we exercised our freedom of choice in favour of a paved road leading more directly towards the Buck's Head. The decision made, Max launched back into his theme.

'God knew everything right from the start when he created the world and gave man the gift of choice, so was fully aware that down the road we would abuse that freedom. Yet he still went ahead and set us free. People have always been to blame for making wrong choices, from Adam's apple to the crucifixion, but God permitted it and therefore is ultimately responsible.'

'Max, I have always wondered what Jesus meant when he said to Pilate: "*You would have no power over me unless it had been given you from above; therefore he who delivered me to you has the greater sin.*" Who was he talking about? Who was it who gave Pilate power from above and delivered Jesus to Pilate?'

'I assume he meant the priests and religious leaders who sent Jesus to Pilate for trial.'

'But if you are right about God taking ultimate responsibility, wouldn't it make more sense to see Jesus' words as a reference to God the Father? It was ultimately God who gave power to Pilate, and ultimately God who did not answer Jesus' prayer for deliverance but delivered him to Pilate. All bucks stop with God!'

'Well, that's a thought. And it ties up with the fact God chose not to answer prayer even while Jesus was on the cross. Jesus' critics prayed in a kind of a way: "*Let God rescue him now if he wants him, for he said, 'I am the Son of God.'*" I imagine they watched to see what would happen, and when nothing changed, no thunderbolts, no voices from the sky, they must have concluded that they were right to condemn Jesus as a blasphemer. God's silence proved Jesus guilty. And when Jesus shouted out: "*My God, why have you forsaken me?*" there can have been no question left in their minds. God's choice not to intervene was the last nail in the coffin of Jesus' reputation. God was ultimately responsible because he chose not to take action.'

At the bottom of a valley, where the golf course crosses the road, a herd of deer grazed contentedly. They didn't even bother to look up as we sauntered by, lost in our conversation.

'A while back you recommended I should read the book of Job. Well, I have read it. In fact, I have read it often over these past months. Do you know what I think must have been poor old Job's greatest trial? It was the time when he wondered where God had gone, his loss of the sense of God's presence. I literally weep every time I read that section where Job says:

> *Today my complaint is bitter. If only I knew where to find him. I would state my case before him. I would find out what he would answer me. But if I go to the east, he is not there; if I go to the west, I do not find him. When he is at work in the north, I do not see him; when he turns to the south, I catch no glimpse of him.*

Job might well have shouted: "My God, why have you

forsaken me?" And, come to think of it, so might I.'

'Was it Job's fault that disaster after disaster devastated his life, which ultimately led him to doubt the presence of God?'

'No . . . Ah! I see where you are going. It was God who permitted it all, right there in the first couple of chapters. God gave Satan specific permission to make Job's life miserable.'

'So you get my point, then. Isaiah quotes God as saying: "*I form the light and create darkness, I bring prosperity and create disaster; I, The LORD, do all these things.*" God was ultimately responsible for all Job's troubles, including his faith loss, just as God was ultimately responsible for Jesus' suffering, including his loss of the sense of God's presence. So is it so hard to accept that God is also finally responsible for your faith loss?'

'But why? Why would God do that to me?'

'Why did he do it to Job? Partly for his own glory and partly for Job's sake. Even Job recognised that. "*But he knows the way that I take; when he has tested me, I will come forth as gold.*" '

We came to the gates at the far side of the park and squeezed through the pedestrian opening at the side.

'Do you think Job appreciated all that as he sat in the ditch, scratching and whingeing?'

'I shouldn't think he did, most of the time at least. God seems to wrap in mystery many of the things he does in our lives. "*The secret things belong to the LORD our God, but the things revealed belong to us and to our children forever, that we may follow all the words of this law*", as Moses once said. And C. S. Lewis had a similar thought when he suggested of God's mysteries that "you shouldn't open envelopes that are not addressed to you". Just why God put you through the wringer is his business, but doubtless he had good reason. Perhaps you'll never know. It may be one of those "secret things" or perhaps just an envelope addressed to someone else.'

'So why are we talking about all this?' I said, kicking a stone out of the path. 'Are you saying that I am doing wrong by seeking to carry the responsibility for all that has happened this past couple of years and that I should allow God to take it?'

'That's right. Otherwise what will it do to your ministry in the future?'

'I'm not sure that I have a future ministry.'

'That just illustrates my point! You see, you are qualified to take neither the credit nor the blame. The credit will make you proud and the blame will make you quit! God is uniquely able to take both the glory and the responsibility.'

'So I should give God all the praise for all the good things and allow him to carry all the responsibility for all the wrong things too. Is that it?'

'Isn't that precisely why Jesus died – to accept the responsibility for wrong? And isn't that exactly what he invites us to do with our sin, to roll it on to his broad shoulders and let him take the responsibility for disposing of it?'

'Max, this is mind-bending stuff!'

The Buck's Head was full of smoke and conversation so we grabbed a smoked mackerel and a ploughman's from the bar and went outside to sit on the wall overlooking the duck pond.

I told Max about my meeting with Peter Larcombe.

'Good stuff! I hope you said yes.'

'Not yet, I haven't. I'm not sure I am in a position to invite others to believe when my own faith has proved so inadequate.'

'Rubbish! You may not have considered this, but it's just possible that you are the best-qualified evangelist in the country.'

'That's an attractive thought, Max, but just how did you arrive at it?'

'Simple, really. An evangelist helps unbelievers believe. You have struggled in the twilight zone somewhere between faith and unbelief. You can sympathise better than most with the difficulty of believing.'

'That's just what Peter Larcombe said to me an hour ago. I suppose you are going to tell me next to preach faith till I have it.'

'What?'

'Just something someone said to John Wesley.'

'OK. But what I was thinking was that your doubts might make you much more sensitive to the struggles of unbelievers and even make you more credible to them as well. While I was in hospital following my accident, there was a time when I almost lost hope that I would ever be able to walk again. I used to lie there and fantasise about walking through Knole Park. Then reality would reduce me to tears of hopelessness. If an athlete had come to extol the wonders of jogging, it would have plunged me further into the gloom. I would never be like him. But it would have been very different if an ex-paraplegic had hobbled in and said: "Six months back they said I would never walk again, but this morning I took a limp through Knole Park." Surely it is not so very different for the average agnostic who has little hope of believing in God? A glowing

Christian with a bullet-proof faith will irritate him, just as an athlete might have irritated me. But someone who struggles on the borders of faith and doubt might well prove an enormous encouragement.'

'So if I were to accept Peter Larcombe's invitation, what would I say? I really am a little disillusioned with the quick-fix faith peddlers. "Preach faith till you have it" – that seems to be my motto for the day. But what kind of faith can I preach?'

'Something solid that people can get their teeth into,' said Max, biting into a pickled onion.

'Rock solid, more like this wall we are sitting on than your lunch, Max. Rock. Jesus said that to obey him was like building on rock. God wrote the ten commandments on slabs of rock. I think for me it was the sheer wisdom and rightness of God's laws that restored to me the desire to believe. While we were at that church in San Diego I was blown away by the attractiveness of the lifestyle that the Bible seems to define. There was no appeal to my feelings, no demand that I believe a magic show of miracles, no weird mystery that an elite few were in on, leaving the rest of us wondering what we were missing. The emphasis was simply: this is what God has always told us is the right way to live and this is why it makes sense. That was a far more rock-like foundation on which to rebuild a shattered faith than the sand of someone else's subjective experience.'

'Faith has much more to do with action than feeling.' Max fumbled in his pocket and fished out a dog-eared pocket Bible. Eventually he grunted after thumbing his way through most of the New Testament. 'Here. Listen to this:

Not everyone who says to me, 'Lord, Lord,' will enter the

kingdom of heaven, but only he who does the will of my Father who is in heaven. Many will say to me on that day, 'Lord, Lord, did we not prophesy in your name, and in your name drive out demons and perform many miracles?' Then I will tell them plainly, 'I never knew you. Away from me, you evildoers!'

'It seems that *"doing the will of my Father who is in Heaven"* does more to impress Jesus than the exercising of miraculous gifts.'

'So you can recognise genuine faith not so much by a person's ability to work miracles as by his willingness to obey. That makes sense.'

'Yes, but it's this *"Lord, Lord"* reference that seems to me to be significant.' Max pounded his Bible like a preacher and attracted a few strange looks from some of our beer-sucking neighbours. He leaned forward and continued in a slightly more restrained manner. 'If I call Jesus *"Lord"* it implies that Jesus is the Boss and I am the slave, Jesus gives the orders and I simply obey him. But if I try to perform a miracle, I become the one giving the orders and God the one who is expected to obey. "In the name of Jesus I demand that this person be healed!" That makes me sound like the one who gives the orders – the Boss – and God like the one who does my bidding – the slave. Therefore, if faith is the power to move God to act in answer to my prayers, then faith would make me the Boss and God the slave. That is obviously wrong. So genuine faith must be the other way round.'

'Max, you are a genius. They should make you a professor of theology. I think you have touched on some-thing very significant for me. You see, the faith I lost is a faith I never want to find again. It was the kind of faith that seeks to manipulate God to do my bidding; a faith that feeds on miracles and answered prayers; a faith that vanishes like a mist when God declines to obey my requests. But the nature of the faith that seems to be replacing it is obedience. He is the Boss; I am the slave.'

'Wait,' said Max, holding up his hand. 'Don't say another word. I have a thought and I must find it.' I waited in obedient silence while he hunted through the Gospels. 'Here! This is what you mean, isn't it. This is Jesus talking:

Suppose one of you had a servant ploughing or looking after the sheep. Would he say to the servant when he comes in from the field, 'Come along now and sit down to eat'? Would he not rather say, 'Prepare my supper, get yourself ready and wait on me while I eat and drink; after that you may eat and drink'? Would he thank the servant because he did what he was told to do? So you also, when you have done everything you were told to do, should say, 'We are unworthy servants; we have only done our duty.'

'That's it, isn't it? If God never answers another prayer we offer, we should still trust him simply because he is the Boss and we are the slaves. The fact that he does do stuff for us is gravy, but never to be demanded.'

'Lend me that,' I said, grabbing his Bible. 'Where is that passage about the Centurion with the sick servant?' We found it, between us. 'The Centurion seemed to hesitate to put Jesus to any trouble. "*Lord, don't trouble yourself, for I do not deserve to have you come under my roof.*" And he seemed to appreciate the nature of the relationship between master and servant – "*For I myself am a man under authority, with soldiers under me. I tell this one, 'Go,' and he goes; and that one, 'Come,' and he comes. I say to my servant, 'Do this,' and he does it.*" But this next verse puts the icing on the cake: "*When Jesus heard this, he was amazed at him, and turning to the crowd following him, he said, 'I tell you, I have not found such great faith even in Israel.'* " Jesus recognised that kind of obedience as outstanding faith. So genuine faith leads to obedience, rather than convenience.'

'That's it, Justyn. God isn't there just to make our lives easy, answering every prayer we mutter every time something goes wrong. "O God, I need to find the car key so I can get home on time. Show me where it is!" Of course, we can pray about those things, but what happens when the key does not materialise? Is God not real? "O thank you, God, for providing a parking meter right outside the store I need to visit. Isn't God good?" Yes he is, but what do you say next time, when there is no place to park for miles? The fact is God is good whether or not I find my key and a place to park the car.

'Job insisted that even if God should kill him, he would still trust him. Shadrach, Meshach and Abednego told the king who was hell-bent on frying them alive that God was able to rescue them, "but even if he doesn't, there is no way we will break the second commandment by worshipping an idol". Habakkuk testified: "*Though the fig tree do not blossom, nor fruit be on the vines, the produce of the olive fail and the fields yield no food, the flock be cut off from the fold and there be no herd in the stalls, yet will I rejoice in the Lord.*"

'You're right, Justyn. Faith results in obedience, not necessarily in convenience.'

'Hey, Max, you're quite the preacher! Remember my favourite sermon about Peter walking on the water? His great faith was one hundred per cent obedience from his perspective. "Come!" Jesus ordered, and Peter jumped out of the boat and went. It certainly wasn't convenient and I doubt if it felt good. He probably felt heavy and out of place. But he still did it. And it certainly wasn't his faith that stopped him sinking. That was something weird that Jesus did with the water. No, Peter's faith simply made Peter obey.'

'Max, have we struck something new with all this?'

'It's not new. Perhaps it's new to us. But the great men of faith in the Bible always had this kind of faith. Abraham was the father of all who have faith. And he didn't get that reputation because he sat on his duff in Ur of the Chaldeans and waited for the right feelings! He obeyed and went.'

'Do you think it was raw obedience that made him go, or was it because he believed God's promises of huge blessing?'

'It must have been both. He obeyed the command because he believed the promise. But I would guess that he was always conscious that obedience was his part of the bargain, while keeping the promises was God's. When God told him to sacrifice Isaac, Abraham obeyed. He laid the lad on the altar and raised the knife. All the good promises of God were represented by Isaac. But God had told him to sacrifice the promises on the altar of obedience. So Abraham was prepared to burn the promises in obedience to the command.'

'But Abraham only fulfilled his part of the bargain

because he trusted God to keep his. He dared obey only because he trusted that, even if he killed Isaac, God would still find a way to keep his promise.'

'That's my point. His faith inspired ridiculous obedience.'

'Bogus faith plays safe, staying home till God acts. Real faith takes risks, takes obedient action even when it looks like suicide, or perhaps murder, in Abraham's case. What do you think would have happened if Abraham had doubted, as I did? What if he fudged the Isaac sacrifice?'

'Well, he did doubt earlier in the story, and the consequence was Ishmael. Yet God eventually found a way to lead Abraham to genuine faith, the kind that obeys.'

'Yes, and going back to my hero, Peter. He may have had great faith when he stepped out to walk on the water, but before too long he sank, just as I did.'

'But tell me this, Justyn. When was Peter the most safe – while he was walking in faith, or when he was sinking in doubt?'

'You gave me the answer to that, way back on Salisbury Plain. You told me to forget faith and to concentrate on God's faithfulness, knowing that even if I were faithless, he would remain faithful. So the answer to your question is that Peter was safest when he doubted, for it was then that Jesus grabbed him and held him tight. Peter's moment of doubt taught him that God is unchangingly faithful.

'And that is the greatest thing I have learned in my moment of doubt. I am safe in God's faithfulness. No matter how doubting or unfaithful I may be, God will never be anything other than totally faithful to me. I am safe. I am loved. No fear.'

* * *

We went on talking for hours, till all the other customers had gone and we were beginning to get worried about being late home.

When I eventually got home I called Peter Larcombe and agreed to preach. 'I will preach faith till I have it. But I am beginning to realise that I do already have it. So because I have it, I will preach faith.'

13

Hindsight

And preaching faith is what I have been doing ever since.

I wrote this book soon after the events occurred, while they were all fresh in my mind. Twenty years have passed since then, twenty years of Christian ministry.

Peter Larcombe's invitation resulted in an evangelistic series called 'Green Hill'. I recall the terror with which I stood up to speak on the first night. But the words did come, as did the people, hundreds of them.

The following year we initiated a series of eleven consecutive Saturday night evangelistic meetings in London's Central Hall and the Royal Albert Hall, entitled 'New Heart for the Nation'. It says much for God's grace that he permitted a servant who had doubted his very existence to stand up and preach faith before six thousand people little more than a year later.

I have pastored a church in western Canada, and in recent years I led a team of thirty young adults in a five-year cross-Canada evangelistic mission.

Times change. Hildenborough Hall has gone, but buildings and organisations are not the stuff of which permanence is built. People are. Last week I met a middle-aged man who learned to trust God as a teenager in the days when Quintin Carr, Max and Sue, and Joy and I all worked together twenty-five years ago. What God does in the lives of people lasts for ever.

Broughton Manor still stands, as it has for the past 525 years. That was a rock over which I stumbled. Covetousness rots the soul! Perhaps I twisted the Bible in an attempt to justify my own greed. It's hard to analyse your own motives. '*The heart is deceitful above all things. Who can understand it?*'

My mother was indeed a prophet, for my life to date has been that of a preacher of the gospel, just as she predicted. As was true for Joseph, the prophecies turned my young head, but God's word is stronger than the foolishness of youth and more faithful than the doubts of middle age.

Why has it taken so long to publish this account of a chapter in my life of which I am none too proud? It was perhaps the success of Max's book *Halfway to Heaven* that inspired me to turn my own disaster to positive use. When I gave the original draft to Max to critique, he suggested that I should wait till I could give the book a happy ending! But after twenty years no obvious conclusion has yet presented itself. Just as Max still limps with his individualistic walking style, so those doubts have left scars on my faith, constant reminders of questions to which I never found answers. The 'two-by-four' hasn't hit me for a long time, but there are certain issues that I will not probe, not because I fear them, but because I am content to label them 'one of the secret things that belong to the Lord', an envelope addressed to someone other than me. What kind of things? Well, things that might require me to question or judge others, matters that are perhaps between them and God alone, matters of faith or matters of experience.

I have many friends who hold various faiths and some

none. They are sincere people who hold to their views as passionately as do I. I make it my life work to share with them the gospel of Jesus, with one eye on the sky, lest he return before these friends are safe. Yet in my heart I do not fear, because I trust that God who proved to be so faithful to a doubter like me will in some way extend his mercy to them also. People ask for chapter and verse. I have none. It's just a hope which gives me peace as I strive to share the gospel with unwilling people whom I love. But to ask too many questions would prove unprofitable. I am at peace in the knowledge that God is much kinder and wiser than I am, and therefore I am content to file that issue in the folder marked 'God's secret things'.

Other friends have had unmistakably supernatural experiences of God. My sister Jennifer Larcombe tells of conversations she had with the Lord and even of an encounter with him at the very gates of Heaven when she nearly died. She has prayed for people to be healed and has seen immediate answers. She herself was instantly healed after eight years in a wheelchair, an *Unexpected Healing* as she described it in her book (Hodder & Stoughton, 1991).

My second cousin, David Pawson, tells me of miraculous events which come across as almost daily occurrences in his experience – healings, prophesies, gifts of languages, words of knowledge.

However, such miraculous occurrences are at best rare in my experience. No doubt I could make much of our encounter with 'Fred' when we were stuck in the motor home by the lakeside. 'Fred was an angel, the kind some have "entertained unawares".' But he looked terribly human to me and used some very human language when he got mud on his cowboy boots.

Max has made an unusual recovery from his paralysis. He thanks God for it, but is careful not to refer to it as 'a miracle'. An answer to prayer? Yes. A miracle? Well, who is to say? Medically such recoveries are uncommon but they do happen.

Hildenborough's purchase of Oakley Farm, which was such an embarrassment to me, turned out well in the end. The farm was resold at nearly twice what was paid for it and the surplus covered all those lean months when Hildenborough was closed. Was that a miracle? I don't think so, for the property market in general went up over that period and it would have been surprising if it had not made a return on the original investment. Beyond doubt the profit was God's provision.

But were I to write an exaggerated account of how all these things miraculously worked out in the end, would it really help anyone to find a genuine faith in God? I love to read books which tell of miracles, but I often find myself asking questions about them to which I am generally ashamed to admit. So do I doubt the truth of these things in the experience of others? No, of course not. They are part of the lives of dear friends of mine whose word I trust and whose stories I pass on as evidence of God's power. But for me they are 'envelopes addressed to someone else'. God gives gifts to whoever he may choose, and far be it from me to question his generosity or to harbour jealousy. To Simon Peter's question: '*Lord, what about him?*' he received the terse reply: '*What is that to you? You must follow me.*'

So I continue as an evangelist, one who seeks to help unbelievers to trust the good promises of God. My doubts give me a great empathy with the struggles of those whom I seek to help. And perhaps the unimpressive stature of my faith makes the threshold of faith more accessible, just a small step, no bigger than a mustard seed.

The other day I took another walk through Knole Park with Max, twenty years since that first walk and lunch at the Buck's Head. The rain was lashing down last week, so we didn't sit on the wall by the duck pond. Instead we huddled by the fire inside. Max has done well. He never doubted God, even though he went through much deeper waters than did I. He has spent those years preaching the gospel, and has written several books.

Knole Park has not fared so well in the intervening years, for in 1987 devastating winds blew down most of the beautiful trees.

I took the opportunity of being back in England to visit Freda, an old friend of mine in her eighties. We went for a drive and I took her first to Hildenborough Hall. I was anxious to see if the tree where first I received Jesus had suffered the same fate as those in Knole Park. But there it still stands. I parked as close to it as possible, Freda not being very steady on her feet.

'It was by that tree that I made the most significant choice of my whole life,' I told Freda.

'What was that, dear?'

'It was there I asked Jesus to come into my life, when I was only six years old.'

'That's nice, dear.'

'Did you ever do that, Freda?'

She looked wistful. 'No dear, I never did.'

'Well, it's not too late, Freda. Would you like to ask him to come in now?'

'I wouldn't know how. What would I say?'

'This is what I said. It was the words of a children's chorus. "Into my heart; into my heart; come into my heart, Lord Jesus. Come in today. Come in to stay. Come into my heart, Lord Jesus." ' Freda repeated the words along with me and registered the most important choice of her life. I had been only six, while Freda was eighty-six. Faith is simple enough for little children and old ladies to grasp. Why ever did I let it become so complicated?

14

A Walk on the Sea

The wind blasted in my face as the storm whipped up the waves all around me into a frenzy.

'Come! Get out of the safety of your boat and walk on the water to me!'

Faith agreed.

But the storm was very fierce and I couldn't ignore the waves. After a few steps I sank. My friends in the boat feared, while some smirked. I was as a wave of the sea, driven and tossed by the wind. With nothing firm to set my feet on, I was unstable in all my ways. In that condition, what help could I expect?

'Save me!' I cried.

Unexpectedly a hand caught me, lifted me up and set my feet on solid ground.

Now I am back in the boat. If he calls again I may have to go for another walk. The likelihood is that I will sink as before, but I am not afraid. For now I know he'll never let me drown.